# A Guitarist's
## FAQ

Published by
SMT ®,
An imprint of Bobcat Books Limited,
14-15 Berners Street,
London W1T 3LJ, UK

Exclusive Distributors:
Music Sales Limited
Distribution Centre, Newmarket Road,
Bury St Edmunds, Suffolk IP33 3YB, UK
Music Sales Corporation
257 Park Avenue South, New York, NY10010
United States of America
Music Sales Pty Limited
120 Rothschild Avenue,
Rosebery, NSW 2018, Australia

Order No. SMT2145
ISBN 1-84609-499-2

Book layout by Artemis Music Ltd (www.artemismusic.com)
Printed in the EU

Your Guarantee of Quality
As publishers, we strive to produce every book to the highest commercial standards. The music has been freshly engraved and the book has been carefully designed to minimise awkward page turns and to make playing from it a real pleasure. Particular care has been given to specifying acid-free, neutral-sized paper made from pulps which have not been elemental chlorine bleached. This pulp is from farmed sustainable forests and was produced with special regard for the environment. Throughout, the printing and binding have been planned to ensure a sturdy, attractive publication which should give years of enjoyment.If your copy fails to meet our high standards, please inform us and we will gladly replace it.

**www.musicroom.com**

# A Guitarist's
## FAQ

David Mead

# BY THE SAME AUTHOR

Rhythm
10 Minute Guitar Workout
100 Tips For Guitar
100 Tips For Acoustic Guitar
100 Tips For Blues Guitar
Basic Chords
Basic Scales
Basic Workout
Martin Taylor: Autobiography Of A Travelling Musician
Chords And Scales For Guitarists
Crash Course Acoustic Guitar
Talking Guitars
10 Minute Acoustic Guitar Workout
24 Hour Acoustic Guitar

All titles available on SMT via Music Sales

www.davidmead.net

# CONTENTS

# WHAT THE FAQ?

When I took my first steps in what has turned out to be a 30 year long musical journey, many years ago, I had a head full of questions about guitars, learning to play, doing gigs and loads more besides. In fact, there were questions I didn't even know I'd end up asking back then. In those days, we learned by trial and error, which meant going up quite a few blind alleys, causing a lot of frustration and costing a lot of money in terms of buying the wrong gear, or just making some ill-advised career decisions. There was no one around to consult – there were no guitar teachers teaching electric guitar and the whole business of playing 'popular' music for a living – or even for fun – was still such a new and unproved concept that you couldn't trust the answers you got even if you found someone to ask!

Things are different today; now we have colleges where you can go and study for a degree in jazz or rock, or whatever. We have magazines dedicated to learning the instrument, books, DVDs, computer courses, live internet guitar lessons and everything else that the technological revolution can throw at us. But people still want their questions answered – and the nature of those questions hasn't really changed much over the years.

During my career, I've been involved in teaching, magazine journalism, writing and performing – and nowadays take the role of *Guitar Techniques* magazine's agony uncle – The Theory Godmother – answering readers' queries about music theory, gear and how to make music using it.

When I set out to write this book, I thought it would be a good idea to include a cross section of guitar playing related FAQs from right across the board in a sort of chronological order – right from buying your first plectrum to recording a CD. And so that's the content of the book you hold before you now. I didn't rely solely on my own knowledge and experience exclusively, either – I mean, I've covered a lot of ground, musically speaking, but I haven't done everything. So I asked some good friends in the business to shed some light on those specialist areas – music management, publicity, running a pro band, staying out of trouble from a medical point of view, and more besides.

I've tried to cover all the major areas that cause concern to curious guitarists everywhere and in doing so I hope this book will serve as a good read and a valuable resource at the same time.

**David Mead**
Summer 2007

## Acknowledgements

Thanks for the invaluable input from the experts whose services I enlisted, who were (in alphabetical order):

Dr James Cameron
Bruce Dickinson @ BIMM
Phil Hilborne & Laurie Wisefield
Martin Holmes
Brian Kettle
Kenneth Knussen
Stuart McLean
The Musicians' Union (Keith Ames)
Tim Orchard
Alex Pym
Slim from The Hamsters
Tony Skinner @ RGT
James Taylor @ P3 Music/The Guitar Label
Sue Williams @ Frontier Promotions

My thanks also to the musicians whose interviews I have quoted during the course of this book:

Jennifer Batten
Rick Derringer
Mike Keneally
Dominic Miller
Tim Renwick
David Rhodes
Darryl Stuermer
Phil Taylor

Lastly – and certainly not leastly – thanks to Neville Marten and Cliff Douse at *Guitar Techniques* for giving space every month to the diva that is the Theory Godmother. To all at Sanctuary/Music Sales who provide the means to publish my various ravings. My students past and present for asking many of the questions herein and to that invaluable support group of friends, fellow musicians, teachers and sundry wayfarers who have helped me form the answers. To my sons who aren't really sure exactly what it is that dad does for a living, and to Carol who makes sure that I do whatever it is with all the love and support she can muster.

# 1: IN THE GUITAR SHOP

*We begin our journey in the guitar shop. To the seasoned player, such an establishment might represent an 'Aladdin's Cave' of delights, but to the beginner it's often a case of serious option anxiety which all too often ends with an ill-advised impulse purchase...*

**Q:** With such a bewildering array of instruments on the market today, how can a newcomer buy with confidence?

**A:** The answer here is down to research. There are plenty of magazine titles on the shelves that feature reviews of instruments and this would seem a very good place to begin familiarising yourself with the general marketplace. Apart from that, there is the internet which boasts many forums dedicated to guitar playing and I'm sure that a few well aimed questions would be answered courteously by the community at large there.

Research the 'big name brands' and check out some company websites so that you become conversant with model names and general specifications, make up a shortlist of models that you think you would like to try and actively seek them out in shops. Be prepared to travel around a bit as you almost certainly won't find everything you're looking for in a single retail outlet. Ask questions of the sales personnel – a lot of the stories you hear about music shops being staffed by rude, ill-informed would-be megastars is largely unfounded, particularly if the shop has a reputation to protect!

Another source of information is from players themselves. These days it's practically impossible not to know someone who plays guitar, so seek them out and quiz them as to the plus and minus points of particular guitar types and makes.

If you go to gigs locally, see if you can track down the guitarist during a break or afterwards and ask some pointed questions.

Basically, remember that knowledge is power and the better informed you are at point of sale, the more satisfied you will be with your purchase.

**Q:** I can't play guitar at all but want to learn – this means I can't try guitars out in shops, what do I do?

**A:** Take someone with you who can play. It's worth asking even a friend of a friend to go along with you so that you can hear what the guitar sounds like when it's being played properly.

Failing that, most of the staff in guitar shops can usually play and I'm sure they wouldn't mind helping you choose by playing all their favourite licks for you on a number of different guitars while you make your mind up.

When I was teaching full time, I used to offer to go along to shops with my pupils if they were at all unsure about buying something because it was in my interests that they ended up with something appropriate in their hands, too!

**Q:** I want to buy a mid-price acoustic guitar – are there any pointers you can give me?

**A:** My advice would be to seek out a guitar shop that specialises in acoustic guitars so that you have the widest possible choice in a single location, making it easier to carry out side-by-side comparisons. Also, if the shops deal with acoustics exclusively it's more likely that the staff will be better informed and more able to help you in answering questions.

Once again, research will pay dividends here and so spend some time roaming the internet so that you can make a better decision once you have an instrument in front of you.

These days, manufacturing techniques have improved to the point where you can pretty much buy with confidence, especially from reputable specialist stores and so your choice can be made almost purely on feel and sound. Remember that the only way to really hear what an acoustic guitar sounds like is from a few feet away, so get someone in the shop to strum a few chords while you stand back and listen.

**Q: How often am I meant to change strings on my electric guitar?**

**A:** It's impossible to give an accurate estimate here because string wear is governed by a lot of different variables. First and foremost it can be down to how often you play – and how 'heavy handed' you are, too. Obviously someone who beats merry hell out of the strings with wildly strummed chords is going to wear out a set of strings before someone who is a lot more delicate with their noodlings!

String wear is caused by several different factors, too. For a start we're dealing with metal wire kept under tension being subjected to constant vibration and general pulling around from bending or tremolo bar antics and so it's going to begin to suffer from metal fatigue eventually. Add to this the fact that the thin metal from the top three strings and the windings of the lower three are being constantly brought into contact with the metal of the frets – metal on metal – and this is going to start knocking them out of shape. When you put a new set on, all your strings are perfectly round, nicely polished and toned up to vibrate at a specific rate to give you the desired frequency or pitch. After a while, the frets begin to make grooves along the length of the strings meaning that this ability is impaired and tuning and intonation both suffer.

Another factor, believe it or not, is down to an individual's body chemistry. Everyone sweats when they play, but some do so more than others. Sweat attracts dirt and grime and can begin the process of tarnishing quite quickly (which is why you should always wipe the playing surfaces of your guitar down after playing it). So everyone is going to end up with tarnished, out of shape strings which are difficult to keep in tune and sound lifeless and muddy – the trick is to spot when this begins to happen and carry out a string change first!

**Q: How can I date my guitar? I bought it second hand and would love to know when it was made.**

**A:** Many instruments have serial numbers somewhere on the body. In the case of most Gibson solid body guitars, for instance, there is usually a number pressed into the back of the guitar's headstock. On a Fender, it can be on the metal neck plate where the neck joins the body, or on the front of the headstock. Semi-acoustic guitars have labels inside the body with serial numbers on them, as do full acoustics and archtops.

In all cases, these numbers can offer a clue to the date of manufacture – and I use the word 'clue' wisely here because serial numbers were only ever intended as an identifying characteristic at the manufacturing stage – literally so the various parts and pieces of a single instrument could be 'tracked' or identified throughout the process. It's only really since the vintage market opened up (something no one predicted would happen) that they have been used to indicate dates and so on.

A lot of companies have now put this information on their websites and failing that, there are an equal amount of collector sites which have gathered data and are happy to share it.

So make a note of your guitar's number, fire up the computer and go exploring.

**Q: What accessories should I consider buying with my new guitar?**

**A:** I would say that some sort of case or cover is a good place to start, if the guitar doesn't already include one. Possibly a stand, too – a lot of inadvertent damage is caused to instruments by leaving them propped up on chairs or standing against the wall, waiting to be knocked over by the first passing household pet or small person. A stand will reduce this risk significantly, at least.

A tuner is a good purchase, too – especially if this is a first instrument, as tuning can be frustratingly hit and miss without one.

If you're going to be reading music from a songbook, then I'd recommend buying a music stand as I've never been able to find anything that works quite as well and they are comparatively cheap.

A guitar strap is always a good idea, especially if you're going to play standing up at any point, but it's also another line of defence against accidental damage owing to the instrument slipping off your lap whilst practising or playing. Plectrums, obviously, if you're going to use them, and a string winder – a natty little device that fits over the tuning peg of your guitar and saves hours of tortuous wrist turning during a string change.

I realise that this is a long list, but there's always Christmas and birthday present requests from friends and relatives to help you complete it.

**Q: Are electronic tuners a cop out? Surely it's best to learn to tune the guitar by ear?**

**A:** Ideally yes, you should be able to detect if the guitar is in or out of tune purely by ear. But this isn't a facility that develops instantly and so a good electronic tuner is an absolute godsend during the intervening period.

Bear in mind too that virtually all professional guitarists use an electronic tuner on stage – as this can be a highly pressurised (and noisy) environment in which to rely solely on their ears.

**Q: With so many different makes of string on the market today, how do I know which is right for me?**

**A:** Most players find that a certain amount of experimentation with strings is necessary before they settle on a particular make. In the end, the choice tends to be highly individual and wrapped up in different factors like feel, durability, reliability, availability and things like that. I would imagine that it's possible to go into a room with about a dozen different guitarists and receive a dozen different answers to the question, 'What kind of string do you use?'.

To begin with, though, I would say that you're probably better off sticking to 'name brands', the details of which will be revealed with a look through a guitar magazine or two, or a read through some of the guitar forums on the internet. In general, too, it's advisable to avoid cheap strings as they invariably let you down in the end.

**Q: I'm a bit confused about string gauges – how do these affect your playing?**

**A:** Well, let's think about the physics involved, to begin with. Strings 'work' because you have a piece of tensioned wire tuned to pitch and vibrating in space. On an acoustic guitar, this vibration causes the air inside the body of the guitar to move and produce a sound (there are other factors involved here, but I want to paint a simple picture!).

In the case of an electric guitar, the string's vibration excites an electric current from the pickup which is then transferred to an amplifier to make the sound loud enough to hear, often from several galaxies away.

So, at a very basic level, you can see that the thicker the piece of wire is, the more sound will be produced – more air moving about in an acoustic and more excitable electrons on an electric.

So the main factor here is volume – with the added advantage of enhanced tone or timbre, too. If you experiment, you'll find that a set of .010–.046 gauge strings sound 'meatier' on an electric than a set of .008s, for instance. Similarly, a set of mighty .013s will sound a lot more manly than a set of .010s on an acoustic.

So, better tone, more volume – what are the downsides? Obviously, heavier strings are more difficult to bend, and so if you play electric blues and bending is very much a part of your style, you may either have to effect a compromise with your string gauge, or go work out down the guitar gym!

Players who upgrade to a heavier gauge of string often find that they are back in sore finger valley for a while, too – but most will agree that this minor inconvenience was to their advantage as a musician. If you want a general rule, I would say that you should go with the heaviest gauge you can as the improvements in timbre alone are worth the trip. Remember though, that your guitar might need a few tweaks from a qualified technician so that it can cope with the additional string tensions involved.

**Q:** What's a truss rod?

**A:** Very basically speaking, a truss rod is a length of metal that is inserted into the neck of a guitar at point of manufacture in order to strengthen it and counteract the 'upwards' pull of the strings.

Guitar necks are usually made from stiff and durable woods like maple or mahogany, but the constant tension created by the strings tends to want to pull the neck into a bow shape. The truss rod is adjusted so that the neck resists this pull and remains straight – something that is essential for today's electric guitars with low to super low playing actions. There is a level of adjustability, meaning that the truss rod can be tightened or loosened so that the tension of the strings is precisely counterbalanced – but one word of caution; even if your guitar's handbook tells you how to adjust the truss rod on your guitar, don't, as it's a job for a specialist and unskilled meddling will only result in tears before bedtime!

**Q:** I keep reading about players who say that they have 'upgraded' their guitars – what are they talking about?

**A:** To some players, guitars are a bit like cars – the temptation to supercharge, customise or hot-rod their favourite axe is irresistible. Manufacturers have caught on to this idea and so virtually anything you can unscrew from a guitar can be replaced by the 'go faster' variant. Pickups, tuners, trem blocks, bridges and more are all subject to upgrading – sometimes it makes a practical difference, sometimes it's just for show and sometimes, it's the response to snake oil adverts insisting that your guitar will sound or feel better because of an expensive little gizmo you just can't resist. Proceed with extreme caution...

**Q:** What does 'retro-fit' mean?

**A:** Literally anything that is fitted to an instrument after purchase. Can be confused with 'upgrading' (see above).

**Q:** What's the difference between a humbucking pickup and a single coil?

**A:** Single coil pickups – such as the ones that you're most likely to find on a Fender Stratocaster, for instance – comprise six metal slugs which are magnetised and wrapped with copper wire so that the vibration of the string produces a small electrical current. This type of pickup – or some kind of variation upon it – was standard on electric guitars up until the late 50s, when the Gibson guitar company developed the humbucker.

The problem with single coil pickups is that they tend to be noisy and prone to interference from other electrical devices (strip lighting is a real nuisance for single coil users, for instance) and so it's not unusual to find all sorts of buzzes and hums coming from your amp when a single coil is employed.

Cosmetically, a naked humbucker looks like two single coils side by side – but the metal slugs are magnetised so that six of them are in 'north/south' configuration and the other set are 'south/north' which has the effect of cancelling out much of the outside interference thanks to the magic of electronics which we really needn't bother exploring here.

Sound-wise, single coils are bright, bell-like with quite a lot of 'cut', whereas humbuckers tend to be darker and more powerful sounding. As a rule of thumb, the definitive single coil sound is that of the Stratocaster, while the humbucker can be heard doing its thing equally splendidly on a Les Paul.

**Q:** Does the role played by the various bodywoods on an electric guitar make much of a difference to its tone?

**A:** Yes, although be prepared for that difference not to be too shriekingly obvious. In almost exactly the same way that a wine taster will rant on about 'plumminess' and 'a fruity bouquet with a hint of tarmac' many of the actual sonic implications of the various tonewoods in use on electric guitars are unbelievably subtle and usually only detectable by an elite, who have exchanged a rich social life and plenty of friends for a twilight and almost solitary existence reviewing guitars for magazines.

Certain sought-after woods, like seasoned Honduras Mahogany (which is now an endangered species and not generally available), are thought to produce the best possible tone in classic Les Pauls, whereas Alder or Swamp Ash is the bodywood of choice for a Stratocaster. But the simple truth of the matter is that I have personally played

some classic guitars that follow this particular recipe and found them to sound like absolute dogs. Alternatively, I have witnessed gigs where players have wrenched an unbelievable sound from a far more humble range of timbers.

In other words, if I have formed any conclusion at all from my years reviewing guitars, it is that it's not so much one or two individual elements on an electric guitar that make for five-star sound, it's the sum of the parts overall. I've often played two identical models side by side and rarely found the same characteristics emanating from both – there is always some *je ne sais quoi* involved somewhere.

So, body woods should certainly be taken into account, but not considered of prime importance – more vital is the way a guitar feels, sounds and responds as a complete instrument.

**Q:** I keep seeing guitars that appear very similar in design but the price difference is enormous – what's going on, exactly?

**A:** We could be talking about a number of different factors at work here. To begin with, there are certain designs which have been copied virtually to death and so you're certainly likely to see instruments of similar shape and look all over the place and, as you say, at various price points. In many ways it would be true to say that 'you get what you pay for' – especially in the instances where you have the choice between two seemingly identical instruments but one is six times the price of the other.

Common sense should tell us that the more expensive of the two must have certain advantages over the other, despite this factor not being immediately apparent. Closer inspection and a quick audition through an amplifier will probably reveal a lot more – the cheaper of the two is likely to sound thinner and feel generally 'rougher' than the other, especially when we talk really 'bargain bin' prices.

The actual difference will really be present in materials like wood, pickups, hardware and general quality control – and this will be apparent to a seasoned player. So many novices have been caught out, thinking that they're saving money by buying cheap. In my days as a teacher, there was one particular lookalike that I used to dread seeing in a new student's hands. (Before you ask, I'm too much of a gentleman to tell tales out of school and so we'll just refer to it as 'Brand X'.) This particular model was cheap, readily available and universally unplayable to the extent that the necks were nearly always bent and the body about as unresponsive, tone-wise, as a breeze block. I found out that these particular horror stories were made from 'reconstituted hardwood' which, translated from sales patter to conversational English, means 'sawdust held together with glue'. I'm serious. But people kept buying them through a combination of the fact that they looked the business and yet were cheap. On a couple of occasions I recommended that my students returned the instruments under guarantee and bought something slightly more expensive but wholesome and well-mannered. The company concerned eventually caught on and ceased manufacture... and good riddance.

So sometimes a big price difference between similar looking models can just be down to worthy original models versus cheap knock offs – but not always. Sometimes, companies can make budget versions of their own product range – like Fender with their *Squier* range or Gibson with *Epiphone*. Here, the price differential will be down to site of manufacture, hardware quality and so on, but not at cost to the consumer as they are still very workmanlike instruments that won't prevent newbies from learning to play (which was my principal concern with 'Brand X') because of slack quality control and dubious money-saving initiatives.

Your main ally is always going to be research amongst guitar websites, forums, magazines and other players – this way you will learn to tell the difference between the real McCoys and the Great Pretenders.

**Q:** When a manufacturer says an instrument is 'hand assembled' does he mean it's handmade?

**A:** Not necessarily, no – and the giveaway is always the instrument's price. A totally handmade guitar is always going to be expensive – and we're talking many thousands of pounds – because the actual 'hands on' element is going to be pretty intense. It's time-consuming and highly specialised work and you certainly wouldn't expect it to come cheap. Think of any other area that boasts a bespoke service – a hand-built sports car, or a handmade suit – and you wouldn't expect knock-off prices.

As far as I'm aware, a manufacturer is not allowed to use the words 'hand made' unless the instrument is literally just that. This is why there have been plenty of euphemisms over the years which look similar and mean nearly the same thing, but not quite. The trick is to express the actual degree of human interfacing that an instrument has enjoyed without upsetting the lovely people at Consumer Protection!

If I saw 'hand assembled' on an instrument's spec sheet, I would interpret it as meaning that it was assembled by hand from parts that had been cut using an automated process. If in doubt, ask the dealer or manufacturer concerned and don't accept stammering unsure gobbledegook as a reply.

**Q:** Amplifiers seem to come in a frightening amount of different power ratings – how do I know what I need?

**A:** The whole question of power rating in amplifiers is a confusing one – and we can thank maths for that. The problem is that power rating – which is measured in watts – is not linear (e.g. 20 watts would be twice as powerful as 10 watts), it's logarithmic, which means that an amplifier that is twice as powerful as a 10 watt amp is rated at 100 watts. Now I'd be the first person to say that this is unnecessarily confusing, but unfortunately, we're stuck with it.

So, given that in the wild old world of amplification twice ten is 100, consider this:

**2 x 100 watts = 1000 watts**

Now you can see that amplifiers that are rated at 10, 20, 30, 50 or 100 watts aren't in fact covering quite as much ground as you perhaps once thought.

I'm guessing that what most people are interested in isn't the actual power of an amplifier, but how loud it is – and that's a different measurement. As far as actual output level is concerned, we measure it in decibels and it's likely that somewhere in the technical specification of an amplifier the actual dB level has been noted – but even this isn't really what we're looking for in order to give us an idea whether a unit is bedroom-friendly or capable of next door neighbour relationship meltdown. The reason here is that if the measurement of your amplifier's dB level has been noted, it's not too much use to us because it will have been done under scientific conditions – how many dB at the distance of one metre, or something like that. Then you've got to factor in the efficiency and number of speakers – two speakers seem louder than just one sometimes because there is more 'spread' to the sound. A bit like the difference between a hose and a sprinkler system, if you get my drift.

Many amplifiers are clearly designated as being 'practice amps'. These are low powered, physically small units which have enough grunt to keep the bedroom poseur happy, but not enough volume to cause anything more than a minor border war with parents and siblings. In theory, at least...

So the whole thing comes down to educated guesswork in the end. Look at the power rating by all means, as it gives you something of an idea of how much snarl the amp is capable of, but the only real proof is to use the amp at volume and let your ears be the judge. Having tested loads of amps, I can tell you that I've played some frighteningly loud 30 watt amps and some surprisingly demure

100 watters. On the other hand, I've been in the vicinity of 100 watt amps so loud that I literally ran for shelter.

Your best resource is the jungle line – check out websites and forums where amps are evaluated and generally chatted about and you'll soon be able to write a short list of amp models and makes that will probably suit your needs.

**Q:** What's the difference in sound between a combo and an amp with a separate speaker cabinet?

**A:** Usually, it comes down to physical size and portability, as combos are smaller and generally car boot friendly, whereas amps with external cabinets are heavy, less portable and more likely to spend time in a van or estate car.

This kind of thinking can translate to sound, too. Combos rarely exceed housing either two 12-inch speakers – or possibly four tens at a stretch, whereas external cabinets theoretically have no upper limit as you can keep on adding cabinets until you begin to rival the Great Wall of China, if you so desire. So really, it's a question of intensity of sound – combos being more 'compact', perhaps, but amps with the multiple speakers arrays implied by external cabs will have more spread, which usually translates into a greater mid range and improved bass response.

Once again, the only real test is to stand in front of both systems and play – but many players will opt for the portability factor offered by a combo, unless they have access to a van and willing hands to help with the loading and unloading.

**Q:** Is it true that valve amps sound better than the non-valve variety?

**A:** This is a debate that used to rage in guitar magazines in days of yore. The argument between the valve and transistor camps was intense, spiteful and surprisingly passionate, too. In fact, some unscrupulous magazine editors would often fake a letter expounding the virtues of one type of amp or the other just to 'gee up' a tired letters page in their magazines. Ahem...

The thing is that in the early days of electric guitar, all amps were powered by valves. When transistors became the new toys of electronic design, builders tried to emulate the sound of valve amps and, mostly, failed miserably because valves do the job of amplifying in one way and transistors in another.

Guitarists voted with their wallets and continued to buy valve amps. But, as electronics became more sophisticated, the sonic capabilities of valve amps became easier to mimic and so a new 'hybrid' technology began to evolve.

These days, I would suspect that a blindfold test would reveal that it's actually quite hard to tell the two technologies apart – in some instances. I wouldn't say that everyone has got it right yet, but it's certainly the subject of much ongoing research.

I'm not going to add fuel to the smouldering embers here; all I will say is that I have used both and still continue to do so. I use a transistor amp to play jazz on an archtop, but prefer the sound of a valve amp getting downright nasty when I fire up a Strat or Les Paul to play blues. It's really down to individual tastes and auditioning different models until you find one that ticks all the right boxes for you.

**Q:** When I told the guy at the local music store that I was confused by all the different controls on my amp, he said I was an 'RFM'. What does this mean?

**A:** OK, I'll try to be gentle here... In the parlance of the music industry – and, I suspect the computing industry, too – RFM is a term directed towards someone who should perhaps, 'Read the Flipping Manual!'. Or at least, something very similar... On the other hand, perhaps you just caught him on a bad day.

**Q:** What's better, the spring reverb in an amplifier or the digital variety you buy in effects units?

**A:** Once again, this is down to individual tastes and almost impossible to quantify simply. There's little doubt that digital reverb is far more flexible and convenient to use in a studio situation, but spring reverb has its own sort of retro charm, like cars with fins or Bakelite.

The advantages of digital reverb are really summed up by the fact that you usually have a whole range of different reverbs available to you from a single compact unit, whereas spring reverb can be a bit of a one trick pony in many respects. As with many things, it remains a question of taste – if you like a sort of 'vintage' blues or rock sound, then perhaps spring reverb is for you. But if you want to stretch out and experiment a little with different textures, invest in a digital reverb.

**Q:** I've been saving up for my first effects pedal – what should I buy?

**A:** To everyone out there thinking how could you possibly answer a question like this, I'd say that you'd be very surprised at how often I've been asked it in the past!

When you think about it, you've probably got a situation where someone has a guitar they are quite happy with and an amp which is good enough for now – and they want to add another texture to their sound. So which one represents the well trodden path?

I usually recommend some kind of external distortion pedal, if the amp they have is small and a little timid, for instance. On the other hand, I might recommend a chorus pedal or even a wah-wah. But the advice that remains consistent come what may is to find a time when your local music shop isn't busy (i.e. not a Saturday morning) and ask to try a few pedals out.

Make an appointment, if necessary. When you get there, don't leap for the one that does something so excruciatingly off-the-wall that you'll get bored with it after about an hour. Pick something that can be used on plenty of songs (which is one of the reasons I say chorus or wah-wah). Take someone with you to act as a sounding board in the shop – preferably someone whose advice you respect and who can stop you from making an unwise impulse purchase – and spend some time going through some pedals.

**Q:** Is it better to use an amplifier's in-built distortion or buy a separate distortion pedal?

**A:** It depends on what you mean by 'better'. Distortion is a funny old business; a friend of mine who is an electrical engineer is aghast that we guitarists actually want distortion in our signal chains at all. Especially as he's been through years of training, learning how to produce a perfectly distortion free audio signal!

In the early pioneering days of rock and blues guitar, the only way you could get an amp to distort was to turn it up until the components inside approached serious overload and produced a distorted guitar sound. Heaven knows why we decided we liked it, but we did and a whole new sound was born. The 'turn it up full' system stayed in place until the early to mid seventies, when the facility to have a distorted signal you could control – termed 'Master Volume' – came onto the market.

This new technology meant that you could have as much distortion as you liked, but at much less of an output level. Many guitarists took to it immediately – and spared themselves premature deafness as a result – but many decided that you just couldn't beat the sound of an amp used at military strength levels of volume.

Over the years, simulated full-on distortion has improved to the extent that a kind of compromise has been reached in that guitarists still play loud'n'proud, but often employ an external distortion unit for that extra jolt in the amp's front end.

To be honest, when I set an amp up to play, I tend to use the internal distortion in combination with the guitar's controls. First, I set a good solo sound by dialling in enough volume and distortion to suit the occasion.

Then I back the guitar off to about 3/4 of its output and test the sound again. What should happen is that the fierce distortion should have disappeared, leaving me with a 'crunchy' rhythm sound. Then I back the guitar off to about three on a ten scale which is where I should be able to find a relatively clean sound. In this way, I can control my guitar sound from onboard the instrument itself and not bother too much with stepping on pedals.

**Q:** What is meant by the term 'action' on a guitar?

**A:** Generally, the term 'action' refers to the height of the strings above the fretboard, usually measured at the 12th fret.

**Q:** Is it true that a low action helps you play faster?

**A:** Not necessarily, no. There are plenty of jazz players out there who play with medium actions – and no distortion – who are lightening fast. In rock and blues I would say that 'legato playing' – meaning that a player relies a lot on hammer-on and pull-off technique – is more prevalent and so a low action would help out here. But I wouldn't encourage anyone to lower their strings as an alternative to working on their speed in the practice room.

**Q:** What sort of guitar would you recommend for someone who is into heavy metal?

**A:** Heavy metal is all about making some kind of fashion statement, in many ways – hence the appearance of all sorts of gothic, angular guitar designs (usually in black) on music shop walls everywhere. Obviously this is a vast, subjective area, but has to be taken into account as part of the purchase initiative, all the same!

Overall, you're probably looking for a guitar with twin humbuckers and some sort of modern tremolo system as this kind of set up will cover most things.

## Q: Is a hard case better than a gig bag?

**A:** It depends. There are gig bags on the market now that are really tough and will protect your guitar from the usual bumps and bruises involved in normal travelling around. Expect to pay a significant amount of money for a heavy duty one with a deluxe amount of padding, though.

Other soft cases won't offer the same degree of protection – and this will be obvious if you pick one up and examine it. If it feels thin and insubstantial then it's not going to withstand any rough handling – so make sure you have a good look before purchasing.

Cases, too, are very varied. Many manufacturers (of high end instruments in particular) will make sure that their guitars come with a custom-fitted case, often made from seriously tough plastic that you could virtually drive a truck over without incurring any damage (although I would advise you not to take their word for it and give it a try!).

Others are more flimsy and appear no more sturdy than cardboard – and once again this should be obvious with a quick feel around.

There are even cases on the market which are designed to fit around other cases – literally a case within a case. They cost hundreds of pounds, look like they are designed by NASA and are aimed at people who travel a lot by air with precious instruments.

Baggage handlers at airports seem to regard the word 'Fragile' as a challenge, rather than precautionary advice...

So the choice in both instances is varied, but it probably comes down to getting what you pay for in most, erm, cases.

## Q: The guy in my local guitar shop told me that reverb was a heavy rock effect – is he right?

**A:** No he's a misinformed prat – shop somewhere else! Reverb is used in virtually all styles from country, jazz, folk, pop to the darkest grunge metal on the planet. It sounds like a sales gambit to encourage you to buy something he wanted to sell you.

## Q: Should I buy a guitar stand, or is it better to put the instrument away in its case every time?

**A:** It really depends on your domestic circumstances. If you are going to keep your guitar somewhere where there isn't a lot of space and you own a particularly rowdy St Bernard dog, then putting the guitar away in its case every time would be a real winner.

On the other hand, if you have the room at home to afford the luxury of a dedicated space in which to practise, then a stand would be fine.

Most stands are robust enough to resist accidental knocks without toppling – and you would possibly benefit from having easy access to your guitar, too.

I've known a lot of students who have resisted the urge to practise merely because they couldn't be bothered to get their guitar out of its case!

## Q: Is it safe to hang a guitar on the wall?

**A:** As long as you invest in a custom made fitting, all should be well. There are various 'guitar wall hangers' on the market that support the instrument just under its headstock which will do the job adequately.

I'd advise you to avoid any bodge jobs or converted picture hanging devices, though as there is nothing as sad as witnessing the damage a guitar endures when dropped from a height.

**Q:** When I said I wanted to try a guitar in a shop recently, the salesman told me I couldn't. I was genuinely interested in buying it, but nothing I said could convince him to let me play it.

**A:** He didn't tell you that reverb was a heavy rock effect, too did he? (See opposite.) Guitar forums across the world buzz with tales of rudeness, poor service and often downright ignorance on behalf of guitar stores – but I remain optimistic and believe that they are very much a minority these days. Let's face it, everyone has a bad day sometimes and takes it out on someone else – and shops with grumpy, uncooperative sales staff soon get themselves a bad reputation. I would guess that this isn't the case in the store you mention and that you just caught the guy on an off day.

Try again – pick a time when the shop isn't likely to be bustling with punters and ask if it would be OK to try a couple of instruments – or try to find out if there is a time when it would be more convenient. If you still get the brush off, simply take your custom elsewhere as this is the only way we're going to stamp poor service out.

**Q:** When you're buying a guitar is it advantageous to hear it through an amp at volume?

**A:** Not if you know a bit about guitars, I would suggest. The thing is that a guitar NEVER sounds the same as it did in the shop when you get it home, no matter what sort of rigourous test procedures you've put it through previously. What you're really looking for in the shop is how a guitar feels when you sit or stand with it – and a few quick knowledgeable glances will tell you if it has been made well. If you want to test it through an amp, you should listen for a good clean sound – if it passes this test, it will probably stay the course once you add gain and volume in any case.

If you are a regular customer, some shops will let you try an instrument through your own gear at home before you commit to purchasing it. The trick is to negotiate reasonable terms so that everyone experiences a win-win situation; you get the guitar you want and the shop makes a sale.

**Q:** Acoustic guitars seem to come in a bewildering range of body sizes, and yet classical guitars are all approximately the same size – why is this?

**A:** Probably the same reason why all violins are virtually the same – because the repertoire they are expected to perform is virtually finite and well established. Composers know the sound range they can expect from a violin and write within its limitations – and the same is true for the classical guitar. Traditional practices within the classical music world mean that these things are unlikely to change, too.

The steel string guitar is often seen as a bastard offspring of the classical variant – I think unfairly. I would argue that the range of music played on a steel strung acoustic is more vast and varied than that of a classical guitar and that certain variations in style and body size are therefore inevitable.

There is a big difference between strumming some chords on a jumbo-sized acoustic and fingerpicking on a parlour-sized model. In both cases the sound and timbre are different and yet both fit into the rich panoply of current music styles.

**Q:** Guitar necks seem to vary enormously between thin and skinny and thick and chunky – is there a reason?

**A:** Not really – it's more a question of style or fashion than anything else. The original guitar necks employed on electric guitars from the 1950s tended to be thick and quite clubby. This was probably because the instrument was still quite new and a certain amount of give and take was still part of the building process. Indeed, most instrument necks were cut individually by hand and not subjected to computer control as with today's generation and so they do, in fact, vary enormously. Let's not forget the fact that thicker necks are more sturdy, too, and will resist the inclination to bend under the duress from the strings.

Once the instrument gained popularity, certain optimums were sought and things settled down a little. But those of us who like 1950s designs tend to prefer clubbier necks and so certain manufacturers accommodate this, especially if the guitar concerned is a 'vintage' design.

During the 1980s and 1990s necks became thinner and thinner – just thick enough to install a truss rod in some cases – and these were sold to the instrumental rock guitar stunt pilots as being optimised for speed. I played a few and got cramp in my left hand from doing so!

So it's really horses for courses – but in many cases vintage and modern seem to be the principal parameters at work here.

**Q:** What sort of extras is it reasonable to bargain for in a guitar shop when buying a new instrument?

**A:** Once upon a time, it was as much as you could do to ask for a new set of strings and possibly the box the guitar came in from the factory so that you could protect it whilst you took it home on the bus. And that was only if you were very lucky...

These days, it depends on the store. Many will offer a 'free set up' – which, as long as the shop knows what it's doing in this respect, is well worth having and arguably the most advantageous freebie for all concerned. After all, it means that the store can be sure that the instrument they've sold you is in prime condition and set up to your tastes – and you know that a final level of quality control has been employed before you take ownership.

Some manufacturers now offer 'package deals' where you get a guitar, amp, strap, lead, tutor book and tuner all in one box, and in some cases can represent a very good deal

(although I would still insist that someone looks over the guitar for you). Some shops do special deals of a similar nature, too – especially around Christmas!

The point is, you won't know unless you ask and as long as you don't expect too much and depending on how much of a wheeler-dealer you are, you might just strike gold.

**Q:** What does a 'set-up' entail?

**A:** When you buy a new guitar, it's a little like buying a suit 'off the peg'. Basically, you might be happy with the design, colour and look, but there is an area of 'bespoke tweaking' that needs to take place before it 'fits'. Add to this the fact that perhaps quality control in the factory that made the guitar tends to be a little superficial in a 'one size fits all' kind of fashion and you can begin to see the value in letting an expert fettle your new instrument to perfection.

Basically, a guitar tech doing a set-up will check that the truss rod is adjusted so that the guitar neck is as straight as necessary when the instrument is strung with your preferred string gauge. He'll check to see that the frets are seated correctly with no rogue specimens that are taller than the rest (which could cause buzzing or choking off) and that there are no razor sharp fret ends, caused either by the wood of the fretboard shrinking slightly since the guitar was made or by bad workmanship at point of manufacture. He'll make sure that the nut slots are cut correctly and that they suit your string gauge, and that the action is set to your preference, too.

Apart from those few nips and tucks, he'll cast an eye over the entire instrument and make any further adjustments that are necessary – tremolo, pickup height and so on – to ensure that the guitar is as playable as it can be when it returns to your grasp. I've had many guitars set up professionally and the 'before and after' difference in feel and handling can sometimes be quite amazing. It's also reassuring to know that an expert has cast an experienced eye over your new purchase to the extent that you know everything is completely up to spec and working properly.

**Q: Can the height of a guitar's pickups make much of a difference to the sound?**

**A:** Yes, it can. Obviously the strings vibrating closer to the pickup's magnetic field are going to produce a stronger signal leaving the guitar, which will show up as being slightly louder through your amp. The thing to watch for is that the magnets themselves don't begin to interfere with the strings' vibration and produce artificial node points which have the effect of giving you impure, hollow-sounding 'out-of-tune' notes.

Another thing to avoid is adjusting your pickup so that the string actually hits it when fretted high up the neck. As with everything, you want to effect a compromise and make any adjustments slowly whilst listening hard through a clean amp. Don't obsess about it, though – the difference is usually quite a small part of your overall sound, when everything else is taken into account.

**Q: When I went to buy a plectrum, I was amazed to find how many different types and gauges there are. What's the difference?**

**A:** Very basically plectrums go from thin (0.44mm and thinner) to super thick (3mm +) and are made from a variety of materials from plastic to metal. Anything that comes into contact with the string is going to make a difference to the tone produced and plectrums aren't immune from this fact, either.

Thin picks will obviously flex when brought into contact with the string and tend to produce a softer attack, whereas thicker picks don't flex and therefore produce a sturdier tone, overall. So thinner plectrums tend to be good for strumming chords and thicker ones for playing individual notes – but, of course, this is a generalisation. The

only way to be sure what is right for you as an individual is to experiment; plectrums are relatively cheap and so buy yourself an assortment and spend a little time going through them. After a while, you'll probably decide on one particular size, shape and thickness by a process of elimination.

**Q: Are thumb picks and finger picks solely for acoustic players?**

**A:** Not necessarily, no. There are electric guitar players who use them, too – and I believe that thumb and fingerpicks are *de rigeur* if you play pedal steel guitar. Always experiment – and damn convention!

**Q: I want to travel with my guitar on a plane – what sort of precautions do I need to take?**

**A:** The first thing to do is to call some airlines and see what their regulations are concerning taking instruments on flights – and do this before booking anything if you can. Depending on security measures in force at the time, you might find one who will let you take a guitar aboard as hand luggage, although this is getting rarer and rarer, thanks to the perceived threat of escalating global terrorism.

If you are resigned to consigning your guitar to the baggage hold, make sure that your case is up to the rough and indifferent handling it's likely to receive. I know not all airport staff take an almost guerilla-like (or even 'gorilla-like') attitude to other people's belongings, but it's always safer to plan for the worst case scenario. So only a case that is 'flight safe' should be considered and make sure that your name and address details are in and on it somewhere, just in case it ends up making an unscheduled journey on its own and ends up 'lost'. Bear in mind that despite baggage holds being pressurised, they're not heated and so the temperature can plummet – two more reasons why your case needs to be up to the job.

A lot of airlines will let you pay a little extra to have the instrument 'hand loaded' – which should be literally what is implied, i.e. put on board by hand and not thrown on with everything else. This is worth considering as it would seem to be another line of defence against damage. It's probably worth stickering the case with the words 'Fragile – Musical Instrument' too.

If the instrument concerned is really valuable – a vintage or bespoke item, for instance – then you could go all out and consider purchasing one of the truly deluxe case covers which are made from light, space age material and fit around the outside of your case. They're expensive, but I'm told they're a good investment if you travel by air a lot.

**Q:** I've heard that there are basically two types of finish on an electric guitar – what are they?

**A:** The two basic types of finish are representative of older and new instrument manufacturing techniques. Originally, instruments have been lacquered or varnished using a cellulose-based substance.

This is fine, but doesn't age particularly well because it's prone to atmospherics and changes in temperature. This is why many vintage guitars have a cracked, glazed and dull looking finish.

Newer production techniques use polyester-based materials which are hard wearing and resistant to just about everything. They keep their shine for years – I have instruments that are 20 years old that still 'shine up' like brand new, thanks to this particular type of finish.

The trouble is, the vintage-fancying market much prefer the more 'aged' appearance of cellulose (much, I believe, to contemporary instrument manufacturers' amazement!) and believe that this type of finish allows the instrument to breathe because it doesn't completely seal it.

Therefore, the wood continues to mature, which affects the timbre of each vintage instrument individually.

**Q:** My guitar is beginning to look tatty – is it possible to have it repainted?

**A:** In general, yes – but the ease and practicality involved in the operation depend on the finish of the instrument involved (see above). When cellulose begins to look 'tatty' it's not necessarily a good thing to consider refinishing it as it implies that the instrument could be a valuable 'vintage' specimen. Refinishing would diminish its value on the collector market and so it might be more worthwhile to change your thought pattern over from 'tatty' to 'shabby chic' and protect your potential investment.

If the guitar is polyester (which is less likely because the durability of this particular finish rarely succumbs to 'tatty') it's a slightly trickier (and messy) job as the original paint needs to be removed in a chemical bath before any new finish can be applied.

So, before making any decision here, it's worth getting an expert to look at the guitar and give you the low-down on available courses of action as there's no going back afterwards.

**Q:** Some guitars come with two pickups and some with three – what are the advantages here?

**A:** Mainly the tonal palette made available. If you think that the pickups are literally 'listening' to the section of string under which they are located and that the timbre produced at these different points is different, it's easier to see why some players prefer having the choice.

It's really down to that most variable of variables – personal taste, and experimentation is highly advised in order to see if you think that 'more is more' or that 'less is more'.

**Q:** Why are some woods used in guitar manufacture said to be 'rare'?

**A:** It means that either the wood is highly figured – that is, uniquely patterned like some of the 'furniture finish' guitars on the market now – or that the wood is from an endangered species like Honduras Mahogany, where harvesting is either banned or very strictly controlled.

The world stocks of even the rare, endangered wood varieties are not exhausted as a lot of manufacturers – particularly in the bespoke market – have still got stock from years back and are storing the wood for use in only the top of the top instrument range.

**Q:** When you see a guitar top made from flamed or highly figured maple are the markings or patterns in the wood itself or does some sort of process bring it out?

**A:** Believe it or not, the patterns are in the wood itself. Careful and knowledgeable finishing will bring out the markings, but all that's happening is that something that's already there is being accented.

**Q:** I keep hearing about how renewing parts of your guitar with higher quality hardware – nuts, trem blocks, springs, carbon graphite bridge pieces, etc. – enhances the tone of the instrument. Is this true or is it just sales talk?

**A:** It all depends on who is doing the talking! Back in the *Guitarist* offices during the 1990s, we coined the phrase 'guitar voodoo' for idle sales talk that was aimed at making potential purchasers believe that something small and simple would polarise the sound of their instrument from naff to fantastic in just the wave of a screwdriver.

The way I figure it is that most of the 'classic' guitar sounds of yore – and in many cases these are the ones we still seek to emulate – were made without any rocket science becoming involved. Classic era guitars were very basic in construction and amplifiers were hand-wired, valve-driven fundamental circuits feeding basic speakers and so why meddle unnecessarily? Sure, if something is

going to make the job easier or more efficient in some way (and locking strap pegs are a good example of a fine idea), then go for it – but always engage the thought process that asks the question, 'Is this really going to make things easier or better – or am I being sold snake oil by clever sales patter or copy writing?'.

**Q:** I've been looking for an archtop for a while now and I notice that some come with wooden bridges and some with metal. Is there a difference and which is better?

**A:** Wood used to be the material of choice for archtop bridges pretty much universally and many players (including me) still prefer the sound they give a guitar.

The only real problem with wooden bridges is that they tend to wear out and sometimes, with the pressure of the strings gradually working their way into the wood, intonation can become very hit or miss. Metal bridges solve this, with accurate intonation and a hard wearing surface, but, to my mind, at the expense of tone. The best thing to do is to try a side-by-side comparison at a music store and see which your ears tell you is the better sound – and go for it.

**Q:** What is meant by the term 'radius' when applied to a guitar fretboard? I keep seeing this and haven't a clue as to what it means.

**A:** The radius of a fingerboard is – put simply – how 'flat' or 'curved' it is, measured from its bass to treble side.

A slightly more technical explanation would be that, when seen in cross section, a fretboard could be thought of as the arc of a circle. Obviously if the radius of that circle was 7 1/4 inches (18.41 cm) this would result in quite a 'steep' curve to the playing surface, but if it was something more like 10 inches (25.4 cm) it would appear quite flat. You can experiment with a school compass and piece of paper in order to appreciate the exact differences involved if you like.

Vintage Fender Strats used to have a radius of 7 1/4 inches and advocates swear by it as the only radius to have – great for barre chords (because it follows an easy curve of the finger) but perhaps a tendency to 'choke out' on serious bends, unless you like a high action. More recent guitars tend towards a flatter radius as a sort of best of both worlds alternative so that barre chords remain comfortable but lower playing actions can be achieved.

It's all basically another matter of taste and what you become used to, and not something that you need to be overly concerned about. As always, the best advice is to play as many different types of neck as you can – you're almost certain to find that one type or other 'feels' more comfortable without the need to resort to the mathematics of the situation.

**Q:** My 11-year-old son has recently started showing an interest in playing the guitar and so I bought him a Squier Strat for his birthday. I've been playing for years and thought it would be great to teach him myself, but our interests in music don't really cross over and so I'm at a loss where to start. I would be grateful for any advice you could give me.

**A:** The great thing about music is that the same basic mechanics are at work under the surface irrespective of style. For instance, you'll find the same kinds of chord arrangement in operation in the music of ABBA, Mozart, Green Day, Led Zeppelin or Megadeath – style is really just a thin veneer on top and really comes down to orchestration.

So, the best way to form a link between your music interests and those of your son is to find a band he really likes and research a couple of licks or songs from magazines or the internet. If you begin to show him how to play the music he really enjoys, he'll be far more enthusiastic when you begin to show him different techniques or scales.

**Q:** I've recently bought a new acoustic guitar, but there's only one strap peg. Do acoustic guitar makers assume we're all going to play sitting down or am I missing something? Players I see on TV and in videos are standing up and playing – does this mean I've got to be brave and take a Black and Decker to my prized instrument to fit another peg?

**A:** Many acoustic makers still only provide a single strap peg on their instruments and, as far as I know, we have good old traditional manufacturing practices to blame and nothing else. Not so very long ago it was conventional to tie a guitar strap onto the guitar's peghead. This was a method that extended to archtop guitars, too, and a quick glance through some pictures from the 1950s will confirm this. I suspect that the onset of solid body guitars and their subsequent popularity changed the way guitarists attached their straps forever. On a solid body, two strap pegs were the norm and the instrument was 'balanced' this way in use. Naturally, the solid wood meant that there was no shortage of places to put the other peg – something that can be a problem on an acoustic. However, a strap peg can usually be attached to the guitar's heel with little or no problem, but before you fetch your drill and try it yourself, I'd advise you to seek the opinion of a pro guitar tech.

**Q:** A friend of my father's recently gave me an old guitar, but it has nylon strings on it, which isn't very rock'n'roll. Can I put steel strings on it to liven up the sound a bit or won't it sound any good?

**A:** It's not so much the sound you have to worry about, as putting steel strings on a classical guitar will almost certainly seriously damage the instrument. A classical guitar is built very differently to a regular steel string acoustic inasmuch as it doesn't have a truss rod to strengthen the neck or any additional reinforcement at the bridge to compensate for the much higher string tension. This could easily result in the bridge breaking away or lifting from the guitar body which would end up costing a lot to put right. My advice would be to make do with nylon strings for now and save up for a proper steel string acoustic – you'll be a lot better off this way around.

**Q:** I've got a couple of guitars – a Strat and a Les Paul – which are both around ten to 12 years old and it occurred to me that both are getting to the age where they could begin to be classified as 'vintage'. My question is, if I start messing around with changing pickups, tuners and so on, would I risk devaluing the instruments in view of their ongoing vintage status?

**A:** Back in my days on *Guitarist* magazine, we used to opine that prestige instruments should come with a log book, like a car. That way, any alterations, servicing or customisation could be properly recorded, along with a note as to who actually carried out the work. This would do a lot in maintaining and safeguarding a guitar's value as well as giving any future owners a complete 'service history'. It might prevent a lot of DIY bodge jobs, too...

Nobody is quite sure how the vintage market is going to react in the future – vintage Strats and Les Pauls from the 1950s still change hands for amazing amounts of money and the prices of some 1970s models are now surprising everyone and beginning to move skyward, too (the seventies were never considered to be anyone's 'golden era', to put it politely). So it's possible that the instruments you see in guitar shop windows today might be the sought after rare gems

of the future – but who can tell? This kind of market is notoriously fickle and not at all guided by logic – for instance, how will a Relic Strat from 2001 be valued in 20 years' time? I don't think anyone would like to call that one!

Incidentally, I've always found it a good idea to make a note of any upgrades or custom work you have done to a guitar somewhere on the body of the guitar itself. On the inside of the lid to the control cavity of a Les Paul or inside the Trem springs cover on a Strat, for instance. This way you won't have to rely on memory if you sell a guitar sometime in the future. Strictly speaking a 'sensible' upgrade – that is, one which would be considered to enhance the instrument's performance or sound – shouldn't detract from its value, but I'd be inclined to recommend that you keep any bits you remove somewhere safe so that the guitar could feasibly be restored to its original condition at some future date, if necessary.

**Q:** I've recently been looking at some seven-string guitars and want to know if there is a convention that states how you should tune one.

**A:** In essence, you can tune the seventh string in any way you choose, but the convention is to tune it to low B – which is the way that most seven strings on the market are configured, in any case. This way, the 'fourths tuning' of the lower strings is maintained which means that scale shapes will share familiar patterns (see music example below). In other words, the notes on the seventh string will be where your fingers expect them to be.

7 string tuned to B E A D G B E

In fact, when the great jazz guitarist Jimmy Bruno first played a seven-string archtop, he said that he could play it as long as he didn't look at the fretboard. In other words, his fingers instinctively continued scale patterns (and some chord shapes too) onto the seventh string, but it was off-putting if he sought some kind of visual reference. Another great jazz player, Lenny Breau, played seven-string guitars that had an extra top A string, as he maintained that it was easier to play both harmony and melody simultaneously this way.

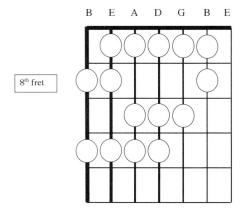

**Q:** I think I may need to change the tuners on my electric guitar, although it's only about three years old. My guitar doesn't seem to hold its tuning at all well and so would such a change improve things overall? I know some manufacturers use cheap hardware on their budget models and so I would be happy to upgrade to a name brand if this would help.

**A:** A guitar repairer friend of mine told me once that the mechanism of a guitar's tuner is so simple that even the cheapest variation will do a passable job – and so it's very unlikely that all six tuners on your guitar have decided to malfunction simultaneously. It would be my guess that there is another problem somewhere else along the line – an improperly cut nut, for instance. I would take it to a reputable guitar tech and have him check the guitar out for you before you consider any hardware upgrades.

# 2: HARDWARE ISSUES

*When all is said and done, a guitar is just a machine – and, as we all know, machines can sometimes malfunction – or, at very least, appear to malfunction. A lot of the time there are a few precautionary steps you can take to avoid unnecessary trips to the instrument repair shop – and some common syndromes to watch out for, too...*

**Q:** I keep breaking strings on my Stratocaster, sending the whole guitar out of tune, due to the pull of the tremolo. I don't really use the trem and I've heard that many players have it disabled – is this a DIY job or do I need to engage the services of a pro?

**A:** No, you wouldn't necessarily need to consult a pro, if you're not squeamish about delving into the guts of your guitar temporarily, at least. Simply slacken the strings of your Strat, turn the guitar over and remove the trem cavity cover. Underneath you'll see two or three springs, connected to the guitar body by a clamp and two screws on the side nearest the guitar's neck. Tighten these up until the springs are stretched and not at all slack and retune your guitar. You should find that your bridge now stays flat on the body – if not, repeat the process until it does. There's a little bit of trial and error here, but when the springs are properly tensioned, you'll find that breaking a string no longer sends the guitar out of tune.

Alternatively, you could insert a carefully proportioned piece of wood between the trem block and body of the guitar.

**Q:** I play a Stratocaster and I'm looking to change the pickups as the stock ones don't seem powerful enough. I'm after a meaty Les Paul sort of sound out of the bridge – what would you recommend?

**A:** The first thing I'd say is if you like the sound of a Gibson, why are you playing a Strat? Getting a Strat to sound like a Gibson is like trying to make an apple taste like an orange! Unless you're really attached to the feel of the Fender, it might be worth thinking about having a total gear 'spring clean' and looking at a second hand Les Paul or something similar.

But if you've decided, for aesthetic reasons or otherwise, that a Strat is the instrument for you then there are various companies that produce pickups which simply slot into place to replace the factory fitted ones. (Well, I say 'simply' but it does involve delving into the guitar with a soldering iron – if your DIY skills aren't quite up to scratch you'd be advised to seek professional assistance!) My advice here is to take advantage of the internet and seek out replacement pickup manufacturers – many have sound samples displaying their wares and so, if you hear something you like, a phone call or email would give you all the information you need. I'd advise against installing anything that means altering your guitar cosmetically, though as this can reduce the second-hand value of it considerably if you are thinking of 'trading up' one day.

**Q:** I've recently moved over to using a lighter gauge string on my acoustic and all is well except for the fact that the A string buzzes like crazy when left open and when it's fretted on the first fret. I've heard that changing to a lighter gauge of string means that you should adjust the truss rod – is this the likely cause of my problem?

**A:** Steady on there! Before you fiddle with the truss rod, take a good look at the nut. If you've changed to a significantly lighter string gauge – say a couple of 'notches' – it's likely that the A string nut slot is slightly too wide and perhaps a little too deep. If the guitar is fairly old, it's odds on that the slots in the nut have worn down a little and, while this might not be too noticeable with your former gauge of string, a lighter gauge will show it up straight away.

My advice would be to take the guitar along to a respected guitar tech and have him check the nut out for you. He will also adjust the truss rod if this is necessary, too.

**Q:** Is it true that heavier gauge strings mean better tone?

**A:** String gauge is a very personal thing and it can take a player years to find one that suits him or her perfectly. The main thing to take note of is that it has to fit in with your playing style; if you have a fairly light touch, then a lighter string gauge will probably work better for you. If, like Stevie Ray Vaughan, you're a very heavy player then moving up a notch or two would be a very sensible idea. Just watch some video footage of Stevie Ray playing and look how punishing his average pick stroke is – if he used light gauge strings he'd be forever breaking them.

It's true that a heavier gauge can mean an improved tonal response through the basic physics principle that more metal vibrating in a magnetic field gives a slightly higher electrical output – in layman's terms, there's more 'sound' to play with. My advice is to experiment a little, but not worry too much about what other players do – you've got to find something right for you.

**Q:** How does distortion work and why did guitarists in the past have to turn the volume to the top so they could get a distorted sound?

**A:** I believe that amplifier distortion was discovered pretty much by accident. In the early days of electric guitar, amplifiers were notoriously underpowered and blues or rock'n'roll players realised that they had

to turn them all the way up in order to compete with the drums or, worse still, the horn section. Amplifier technology was fairly crude – the circuitry was based around valves – and it was the nature of electrical audio circuits back then to distort at high volumes. It was just the way valves behaved once they started operating near the top end of their power capacity.

The odd thing was that guitarists actually liked the way it affected their instruments – it had the effect of fattening the signal and adding sustain, making it sound more like a horn. This was because of the exact way the valves in the circuit distorted the sound – they didn't distort the note itself, but the harmonics of the note were affected and generally 'fuzzed up'. Eventually, amp manufacturers caught on and started making amps with all sorts of adjustable distortion characteristics.

**Q:** I have just bought my first guitar with a modern, floating tremolo system and have found that it tends to lack sustain when played through distortion. Is a set-up necessary or is this something that features on modern trem systems?

**A:** It's true that a 'floating' trem system will affect the way that a guitar sounds and that you will notice a difference between a trem and non-trem guitar. There are many reasons for this, one of which being that the trem springs actually absorb some of the string vibration and can result in a lack of sustain. However, if the guitar is properly set up this effect can be minimised. So my advice would be to take your guitar back to the shop and ask for it to be set up. Alternatively, seek out a professional guitar repairer and get them to look over the guitar for you.

**Q:** I recently purchased an Ibanez with tremolo arm. Being conscientious, and after playing it for a week or so (with no tuning/stability problems), I decided to change the strings. This is where my problems started. The more I tightened the new strings, to get to the right pitch, the more the tension

**pulled up the trem mechanism – which then lowers the tension. So it's a vicious circle of tightening strings vs. losing tension because the trem moves. At the point where the action was raised so high I wouldn't have been able to play the guitar I gave up, thinking that I must be missing some basic point somewhere. Please help?**

**A:** It sounds like you've increased the string gauge – the Ibanez was probably strung with 009s and perhaps you use 10s or 009–046s? In any case it's absolutely normal for a trem type guitar to react the way yours has and all it takes to put it right is a little trial and error with a screwdriver.

If you turn the guitar over, you'll see a plastic oblong on the back held down with six (or four) screws. Unscrew it and you'll see a mechanism inside comprising springs and claws. First of all, if there are only two springs (and Ibanez gave you a spare) you can insert a third as this will obviously help even up the string vs spring tension (which gave you the problem in the first place). If there are already three springs, you need to turn your attention to the two screws at the neck end of the apparatus. If you screw these two in a little – just half a turn at the most each time – and then retune, you'll find that the bridge begins to level off. If you overdo it, release the screws slightly, and so on until the top of the trem is level with the surface of the guitar. It's important that you tune the guitar to pitch in between each spring adjustment so that you can check progress. As I say, this is a common situation with trem guitars but as long as you stick to a single string gauge from now on, you'll only have to do this job once.

**Q:** I'd like to learn about tapping and hammer-ons. I only have a standard Fender Strat and a bottom of the range amp and I can't get the right sound even when I turn the gain right up. What equipment will I have to buy to be able to do this right?

**A:** You shouldn't have to buy any new gear – people can learn to tap on an acoustic guitar and so your Strat is more than adequate. It's probably a question of mastering the technique itself rather than anything else. I would advise you to try some simple experiments on an unamplified guitar to begin with; simply use your right hand index finger to sound a few notes on the top three strings by tapping the frets.

Experiment with different degrees of pressure and positioning until you find that notes sound clear. Then fret a note on the G string with your left hand (any note will do) and tap some notes higher up the fretboard on the same string. If you drag the right-hand index finger off the string very slightly (rather than merely raise it) it should have the effect of gently plucking the string so that it sounds the note held by the left hand. When everything begins working acoustically, plug your guitar in, turn the gain up and try again. This time, you should find that things are beginning to happen. If you spend some practice time every day working away at your tapping and hammering skills you'll see results.

**Q:** I have a new guitar with a tremolo arm. I was trying to pull the bar up and check the tuning stability after that. I noticed on my GT3 Boss tuner that the pitch is raised about two arrows up. When I dive the bar it returns to the right pitch again, but after several times I noticed that it is raising about 1/8 tones which is more than two arrows. But it returns to pitch when I dive. How come?

**A:** There are several reasons why a locking trem system can suffer from tuning instability. The most obvious is new strings that are still 'stretching in' and causing glitches, but if the strings are returning to perfect intonation after 'diving' it's more likely that your trem is in need of setting up.

Before doing anything, check that the locking nut is firm and the strings are seated in the bridge correctly. Then, look along the side of the trem and see if it's parallel to the guitar's surface when in 'rest' position. If it isn't – either 'up' at the back or front, then it needs adjustment, which is fairly simple and can be done with nothing more than a screwdriver and a lot of patience. The exact details are explained in the handbook that should have come with the guitar or on the internet. One thing, though – if this is a new instrument you could always take it back to the shop and ask them to set it up for you.

**Q:** I play acoustic and electric and am satisfied with my electric guitar but find the action on my acoustic too high when trying to play past about the 7th or 9th frets, especially fast lead or sliding with partial barre chords. Is there a problem with my guitar or is this common on all acoustics?

**A:** Traditionally, action measurements are taken at the 12th fret, measuring from the top of the fret to the underside of the string. I have two acoustic guitars, one (a Yamaha LLX 500C) measures in at 2mm (bass side) and the other (a Yamaha APX) at 2.5mm.

I play both of these guitars professionally and find the action very finger friendly in both cases – and neither have been 'tweaked' in any way, they are the same as when they came out of the box. I've also been in the lucky position several times of having the chance to handle other players' instruments and none of them had what I would call a particularly low action on their acoustics.

The thing is that electric guitar players will always find that acoustic guitars are awkward to play in that the action is traditionally higher and the string gauge always heavier – two things which are bound to feel weird to anyone who is more used to .009 gauge strings and micro actions.

If you're still in doubt, take your guitar to a reputable guitar tech and ask his 'hands on' advice. There is always the chance that he could lower the action to give you buzz free comfort if you really can't get on with a higher one. It's probably better to do this before you're tempted to upgrade in any way, too.

**Q:** I recently acquired an acoustic guitar – my first. After years of playing electric, I'm finding that the strings on my new guitar are much too heavy, but my local guitar shop tells me that they don't do a 009 gauge for acoustic and that I should look at trying to get used to a heavy gauge as this will make the guitar sound better. Is this right?

**A:** It's dead right, yes. Unlike an electric guitar where the sound of the strings is taken up by the pickups and amplified, an acoustic guitar relies on the production of its sound via the vibration of body woods and the stimulation of air inside the body – and strings as light as 009s lack the necessary muscle to get that wood singing.

Players who swap from electric to acoustic generally have a problem adjusting from light strings to the heavier acoustic variety and so you're not alone. If you want to make the adjustment slowly, try stringing your acoustic with a set of 010s first of all and gradually work up to 012s. The improvement in tone will be worth all the blisters in the end!

**Q:** My strings keep going out of tune. When I tune up everything seems to be fine, but then when I bend a note there's a sort of 'ping' and the string goes out of tune again. Do I need a new nut? Only the guitar isn't that old, but I did buy it second hand.

**A:** Without examining the nut on your guitar it's difficult to tell if it's at fault or not – although a good guitar tech would certainly see if there was anything untoward happening in that area. But before you take your guitar in for a check up, it's worth considering an alternate remedy.

It's possible that the strings are merely becoming a little 'stuck' in the nut when you bend a string, which results in the open string sounding sharp (and causes the 'ping' noise!). This is a common problem on guitars and generally nothing to worry about. It can be easily remedied with the judicious use of some lip balm, petroleum jelly or a proprietary string lubricant applied to the grooves in the nut to ensure smooth passage of the string when you're bending or using a whammy bar. Try this first – if it solves the problem then all is probably well, but if it doesn't then a trip to the nearest guitar tech will certainly be required.

**Q:** Is it right that you should change strings one at a time rather than take them all off first? If so, why?

**A:** Changing strings one at a time is advisable for several reasons. For a start, it maintains the tension on the neck as far as possible – you're probably aware that the general 'straightness' of a guitar neck is a question of balance between string tension pulling the neck forward on the one hand and the stiffness of the wood, aided by the truss rod, pulling it back on the other.

On some guitars, especially those with thinner necks, this balance can be a little 'hair trigger' and so taking all of the strings off at once can cause problems and show up any minor defects in manufacture. I've known frets pop up from their bedding in the fretboard after an 'all off' string change which causes choking and other horrors that will have you running to the repair shop.

Apart from that, guitar DIY novices can be quite alarmed when bits start dropping off their precious instruments during a change of strings. On an archtop, for instance, the bridge is held in place by the pressure of the strings alone and will make a sudden bid for freedom when this pressure is removed, which can cause intonation nightmares later on.

Some hi-tech trem systems can react horribly if the guitar is totally denuded, too. I once had a pupil of mine arrive for his lesson with his prized Ibanez in two separate carrier bags because a simple string change had gone disastrously wrong. So, unless there is any pressing work to be carried out on the fretboard itself, it's good general practice to change the strings one at a time.

**Q:** My guitar has developed a problem. When I play the B string it sounds like a sitar – there's a definite buzzy twang to it along with the note. I haven't changed the strings or made any other kind of alteration and so I've no idea what's going on. Can you help or should I try to get a gig at my local Indian restaurant?

**A:** First of all it's probably a good idea to change the B string to eliminate the possibility of it causing the problem by being damaged or worn. If the situation persists, it is probably down to wear and tear at one end of the playing length of your B string – either at the bridge or at the nut.

If the string slot in the nut has worn down over the years, your B string could be coming into contact with the first fret – the telling factor here would be if you can hear the 'sitar effect' on fretted notes as well as the open string. It could also be that the string slot has widened, causing a bit of unwanted movement, or that it has some dirt trapped in there, causing interference.

At the other end of the string, check for wear at the bridge. If the string saddle is worn or damaged it could produce this effect, too.

In either case, I'm afraid it sounds like a job for a qualified repairman and not something you can put right yourself.

**Q:** Help! I decided to give my guitar a spring clean and a string change, and so I took all the strings off and cleaned the fretboard, re-strung it with exactly the same make and gauge of strings, didn't touch anything else, didn't move the bridge or anything. But now I'm getting all sorts of string buzz that just wasn't there before – I swear I didn't do anything other than wipe the fretboard down with some furniture polish and put the strings back – so how could I have caused any damage?

**A:** If you took all the strings off your guitar at once, the chances are that the neck bent back very slightly due to the pull from the truss rod – the counter-tension from the strings having been relaxed (see question above). In some cases this can cause a couple of frets to lift out of their slots very slightly so that when the tension from the strings is reapplied they remain high enough to cause the problem you describe.

It's not an impossible situation to put right, given the appropriate expertise, but it's definitely not a DIY proposition. Hasten ye to a qualified guitar tech and your guitar should lose its buzz in no time. Oh, and next time you change the strings, doing so one at a time might be a good idea!

**Q:** I play acoustic guitar and want to start playing my own songs live, but my guitar hasn't got a pickup fitted to it. As I'm really comfortable with this guitar and can't really afford to change or upgrade it, is there a way around the problem or should I start thinking about buying a microphone?

**A:** Why don't you consider having a pickup system installed on your acoustic? These days many systems are on the market that are easy for a professional guitar tech to install and the cost would be far less than an upgrade in most circumstances. You could have an undersaddle piezo and preamp installed or even a soundhole pickup (which usually means less modification).

I suggest you have a chat with a guitar tech and explore the options where pickup systems are concerned as they offer a lot more flexibility than being cemented in place in front of a microphone on stage.

# 3: THE PRACTICE ROOM

*I think that probably the hands-down winner where frequently asked questions with regards to practising is concerned would be, 'How long will it take me to become good?' And the answer, of course, is that you will get out of the guitar exactly what you put into it and nothing more. Learning to play involves practice – we all know that. But in order to advance to what we might term a 'pro' level takes a lot more dedicated time, patience and energy than is often realised. You can bet that when you see some guitar wizardry on stage somewhere, the person responsible has spent literally thousands of hours perfecting his or her craft.*

*The mistake most often made in the practice room is to play everything you already know and not challenge yourself by venturing into unknown territory. This way you never really improve and soon find yourself in a rut. Practising unfamiliar stuff puts you in a very scary insecure place and nobody likes spending too much time there... It takes you back to day one and makes you feel like a complete idiot and you need that comfortable security of going over material you actually know just to reassure yourself that you can still play. So the trick is to balance things out; by all means keep your current repertoire fresh by reviewing it, but remember to input something new all the time, too.*

*Another thing is that there's always a time lag to be taken into consideration with learning an instrument. It's common to find that when you're on page 26 of a tutor you're only really beginning to understand page one! But this is normal; it takes time to assimilate new techniques into your playing and it's perfectly natural to discover that learning to play is more like osmosis than anything else. It's gradual – and advanced skills don't come overnight. So you're going to make mistakes and find certain things absolutely impossible the first time you try them. The important thing here is not letting it matter – expect mistakes and don't see them as a sign of weakness or lack of 'talent'. Just think about how often you fell off your bicycle before you learned to ride. Remember that most skills can be learned, it just means an investment of time and there are plenty of people out there who find it very difficult to make that investment owing to the fact that they lead busy lives...*

**Q:** I don't get the idea of chord substitution at all. How can one chord replace another? Surely it would just sound wrong?

**A:** Chord substitution is an enormous subject and one that is far too complex to go into in a book of this size, but I think it can be summed up in some kind of nutshell.

Let's look at the maths of the situation. To begin with, think of the chromatic scale; that's 12 notes – OK? Now, even if we're thinking very basically, we'd say that there is a major, minor and 7th chord for every note

and so that would give us 3 x 12 which equals 36. Take into account some of the bigger, 'extended' chords like maj6ths, maj7ths, minor 7ths, 9ths, 11ths, 13ths, add them into our equation and you'd now have another 72 chords –and we're nowhere near the bottom of the chord barrel.

In fact, if we factored in every type of chord there is, you'd end up with hundreds – but we've only got 12 notes to use in all of them. So it's natural that many chords use similar notes and when things become very similar, they're often close enough to act as a substitute for each other, as shown overleaf:

C maj = C E G
Amin = A C E

These two chords share two notes and so sound close enough to be interchanged in many instances.

Like I say, this is a huge topic, but these are the basic facts. I'd advise some exploration of the internet for further and deeper insight into the topic – it's also covered in many books, especially in jazz titles.

**Q:** I've got several books on scales, most of which show fingerings which have two notes on one string and three on another – and these are the ones I've been practising so far. My teacher now tells me that it would be best for me to learn fingerings that have three notes per string, which means going back to the drawing board and starting again. I play rock guitar in the Paul Gilbert, Satriani mould – would this other way of playing scales actually help?

**A:** The quick answer here is that both methods are equally valid. Rock phrasing is notoriously triplet based – if you think of the typical rock guitar line having a sort of 'widd-er-ly widd-er-ly widd-er-ly' rhythm, you'll see what I mean. So, bearing this in mind, having three notes per string aids phrasing immensely as one pick stroke per string and some conscientious hammer-ons or pull-offs will give you that rhythmic feel automatically and, in general, will make things flow nicely. But I wouldn't recommend adopting this kind of fingering regime rigidly as it can lock your playing into one rhythmic groove too easily – and that's where knowing the other method for fingering will really pay off.

**Q:** I've developed my fingerstyle technique to a fairly high level, but I'm not so versatile when it comes to using a plectrum. I've always used my index and middle finger (as well as my thumb) to hold it, as I felt it gave me more control and came naturally. I've been wondering if this is holding me back with regard to speed... does it make a difference? If I should be using only thumb and index finger, can you recommend anything to try to get used to it? I've been trying but keep slipping back into two fingers and thumb.

**A:** This is a fairly common problem. I had to correct my plectrum wielding technique at one stage as I used to hold one with index, middle and thumb. So, having been there myself, I can tell you that the answer is practice – and nothing else. If you try to keep the rest of the fingers on your picking hand relaxed – 'fanned out' if possible – it helps. It does make a difference because holding a pick with three fingers can increase the tension in the hand – something that will hamper speed and fluency if left uncorrected.

**Q:** Is there a way of working out a scale that will sound good over a particular chord sequence?

**A:** A song is generally made up from two things: a melody and some sort of underlying harmony. Usually you have a tune on one hand and some chords underneath it. It's tempting to believe at first that this process is wholly arbitrary, but there is a system – and it's stuck to nearly all of the time.

Let's take a scale – C major is always good. The letter names here look like this:

C D E F G A B C
1 2 3 4 5 6 7 1

Here, then, is the raw material for our melody – but what about the chords? They are drawn from the same materials as the scale – they've usually been 'stacked up' vertically so that we're playing chunks of the scale simultaneously. There's a system here, too, in that we use stacked 'thirds' – in effect, this comes down to taking every other note from the scale and superimposing it. The simple chords stop at three notes, though. So, if we apply this kind of thinking, we arrive at a new looking scale:

| G | A | B | C | D | E | F | G |
|---|---|---|---|---|---|---|---|
| E | F | G | A | B | C | D | E |
| C | D | E | F | G | A | B | C |

| C | Dm | Em | F | G | Am | Bdim | C |
|---|----|----|---|---|----|------|---|

Now we have a chord for each member of the scale – we've literally harmonised the scale itself. If you play through these chords, you should still be able to hear the familiar 'scale' sound rising through them.

So, now we have an area from which we can build both melody (the original scale) and the harmony (the 'stacked' version) but it would make our job as rhythm guitarists much too intensive if we changed chord every single melody note. It would also make the music too 'busy' and uncomfortable to listen to, so we use one chord to support several notes at a time. In fact, just three chords from the above 'stacked' scale are enough to support a lot of simple melodies.

| G | C | D |
|---|---|---|
| E | A | B |
| C | F | G |

| C | F | G |
|---|---|---|

You're more likely to see the G chord as G7, but that only means that another note has been stacked above the three we already have:

F
D
B
G

G7

So, from this you can see that both melody and harmony come from the exact same resource – chords and scales are different ways of looking at the same thing. If you were going to form a solo based on the chords C major, F major and G7, you'd use their 'relative scale' which is C major. When you think about it, what you're doing when you play a solo is replacing the original melody with one of your own and so you use the same raw materials.

Obviously we're only really skimming the surface here, but these are the basic principles at work. There are some books out there that will help explain things further – any book on basic guitar harmony should help you.

**Q:** I have been playing guitar for around two years, and have mastered simple open chords. However, I have great difficulty getting to grips with the A-shape barre chord. Ideally, I would like to be able to play this shape using the first finger to hold down the first and fifth strings, and the third finger as half a barre to hold down the middle three strings. Any tips on hand positions or exercises you may have to help me master this infuriating chord will be greatly appreciated.

**A:** This is a tricky chord to pull off in the initial stages of playing because it calls for increased flexibility in the third fingertip of the left hand. This is usually only attained with practice over a period of time – and so patience is the first thing to grab on to!

You might find that the job is made a lot easier if you practise it with the first finger holding down only the fifth string and the third holding the fourth, third and second strings respectively. After the necessary flexibility of the joint in the third finger has been attained, you should find that this works fine.

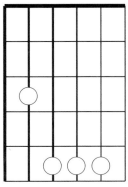

Fingering: 1   3   3   3

**Q:** My musical memory is not very good at all. I can learn a song, scale, or new chord and within a day or two I won't be able to remember it without looking back at the reference. Where am I going wrong? I want to be able to remember songs and scales forever when I learn them.

**A:** The thing about memorisation is that whereas we all learn in much the same way, different people learn at different rates. Broadly speaking, all new information enters the brain via the short-term memory, only passing on to the long-term memory if the brain considers it important enough. This is fine for remembering directions to somewhere in a strange town that you have to visit only once; the information is called upon and then not needed again and so is discarded or overwritten. But if it is a question of learning a route that you're going to be taking frequently, then it finds its way into the long-term memory in order that it is available all the time.

Learning a new chord shape or scale is no different, we just have to make sure that the information is processed correctly and ends up in the appropriate 'long-term' area – and it's this act of 'processing' where people tend to differ.

At one end of the spectrum there are people with a so-called 'photographic memory' who appear to be able to look at something once and remember it immediately. At the other, there are people with an extremely poor facility who have to look, look again and then go back and take a further look before anything sinks in at all! Luckily, most of us seem to check in around the middle, either side of average, although recent research has found that even diet can affect attention span, concentration and the ability to input information.

Experience and techniques involving the new science of Neuro-Linguistic Programming can help improve memory, but on the whole we're stuck with whatever was handed out to us at birth and a lot of us learn at the same rate throughout our lives. In other words, if you were a quick learner at school, then the chances are that you'll remain so for the rest of your life.

What you have to do is take a look at how you learn and set up a practice routine that will move at the correct rate. For instance, I've found that short, regular bursts of inputting new material suits most people the best. Limit the amount of new information you tackle at once – literally feed yourself according to your own particular rate of digestion. Study whatever it is daily, revise it regularly and you should find that new musical data can be inputted successfully and remain useful to you.

Another tip for memorisation involves writing the information down – so called 'pen memory'. I used to recommend to pupils that they wrote a scale pattern or chord shape that was giving them difficulty down on a piece of paper and put it somewhere they would see it every day. Then, after about a week, remove it and replace it with something new, just to keep the brain engaged.

It's worth getting hold of an exercise book and keeping a running log of 'new data'; look at it at the beginning of your practice session, run through everything once or twice for maybe ten minutes and then get on with the business of the day.

**Q:** I keep seeing chords notated above transcriptions in music books that just say 'C alt'. I understand that this means 'C altered 7th' but what does it mean in terms of what notes are being used?

**A:** For the uninitiated, the altered dominant scale contains all of the altered intervals that are part of jazz's common parlance. If we were looking at an ordinary C7 chord, for instance, playing the C7alt scale over it would give us the flat nine, sharp nine, flat 5th and sharp 5th all in one scale. It's about as far 'out' as you can get and sounds very 'jazz' if positioned correctly.

As to the positioning of chords in general, it might be a good idea to familiarise yourself with the CAGED system – there is a mighty amount of information on the internet and several books that will guide you through, if you're unfamiliar with its charms. CAGED really does make the fretboard look far more friendly, both in terms of chords and scale positioning.

**Q:** What does it mean when I see a little degree symbol (°) next to a chord name?

**A:** The little degree sign by a chord means that it's a diminished chord, containing a root, flat 3rd, flat 5th and 6th (also known as a double flat 7th). Because the diminished chord is symmetrical as far as construction is concerned, there are only a few shapes for it – and a good chord tutor will show you all of them.

**Q:** I've got a chord book and it shows loads of different shapes for each chord – often the main difference being that some have three notes, some four, five or six. How do I know which one will work the best?

**A:** The question of how many notes you play in a chord is quite often down to the taste and individual choice of the player concerned – and the line up of the band, for that matter. If you are playing with a bassist it's often preferable to leave out the root of the chord, for instance. Keyboard players tend to fill the harmonic space more than adequately, leaving the guitarist with nothing to contribute and so nothing more than a few scant accompaniment ideas are all that's necessary. Experimentation and experience are the two key factors here – literally try every alternative and keep the things that please you. After all, this is the beginning of building a style.

**Q:** I've been playing the guitar for over two years now and I know very little about the theory behind the instrument. I really want to learn jazz, but I find all the jazz resources available in terms of books, DVDs, etc are very advanced, so how do I go about making this particular journey? Where's a good place to start?

**A:** If you're serious about entering the hallowed halls of jazz it would be a good idea to learn to read music, even if it's only enough to read a melody line. Many of the facilities used by jazz players – like fake books, for example – have no tablature in them as they are written for all instruments and not just guitarists. So learning to read gives you access to a wealth of material.

As far as tutors are concerned, have you searched the internet? There are many sites that have free lessons on jazz – doing a search on 'jazz guitar' should reveal many of them, as well as several 'recommended reading' lists.

If you still want to follow the book route on your own, get hold of a good chord book – something like the *Jazz Guitar Chord Bible* by Warren Nunes would do nicely. Then get your hands on a fake book – a book that contains the chord arrangements and melody lines of loads of jazz tunes – and start working through the chord charts. This will begin to get the basic harmony of jazz into your ear and from there you are free to take things any way you choose.

**Q:** What the heck are modes? I've learnt my pentatonics back to front and know the relatives like Amin and Cmaj, but I keep hearing about modes like they are some kind of Holy Grail of rock music.

**A:** Very basically speaking, the modes represent a medieval approach to music as they originated way back in the Middle Ages. In those days, we didn't have key signatures like we do now, mainly because the instruments of the day weren't in tune to the extent that they could play sufficiently well in more than one. Just after the Renaissance, roughly speaking the 17th Century, music was 'sorted out' to the extent that every note in the scale was 'quantised' so that it was mathematically equidistant to its surrounding neighbours. In other words, C was the same distance from C♯ as F was to F♯.

This made the whole subject of keys suddenly available and composers like Bach took full advantage of this, writing pieces in as many keys as were available. So the 'modal' thinking was abandoned in favour of the new 'equal temperament' system, until composers rediscovered them much later on.

Modality is based on a single scale of seven notes played from its different roots and so, if we take the key of A major as an example, we find that a different sound is produced if we play the scale from its second or third notes. So, playing from A to A gives us the familiar major scale sound, playing the same series of notes from B to B gives us another – and so on.

Each 'mode' has its own unique properties and its own name, too:

I – Ionian

II – Dorian

III – Phrygian

IV – Lydian

V – Mixolydian

VI – Aeolian

VII – Locrian

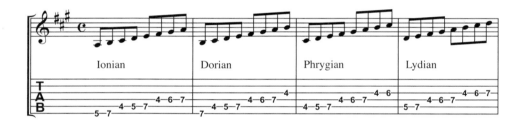

In modern times, certain styles of music have adopted some of the modes as their own – jazz players favour the Mixolydian, Spanish-influenced players favour the Phrygian and so on. You might have heard the rock guitar elite like Joe Satriani or Steve Vai talk about using modes – Vai in particular has had a long-standing affair with the Lydian mode in his music.

It's a big subject and one that is definitely well worth exploring and so here, to set you on the way are the seven modes in A major, presented in both tab and box shapes.

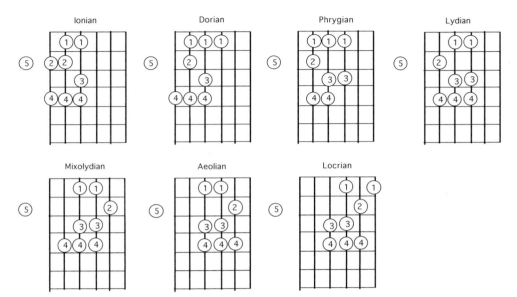

**Q:** I want to use a Mixolydian mode in some blues soloing. The problem is that I know the scale but I don't know how to use it in some good licks. Please help me.

**A:** You wouldn't be the first person to discover that it's difficult to make scales sound like music! The thing about the modes is that it's actually very difficult to hear exactly what's going on without hearing the mode in its correct context. Unaccompanied, our ears tend to hear the major scale played from the middle and not a separate entity like the Mixolydian. I suggest that you get hold of some backing tracks (there are plenty of free MIDI files on the internet – a quick Google should yield bountiful results) and play the scale over them. With luck, your ear should begin to catch on and you'll find some new licks coming your way straight away.

**Q:** In many songs I see chords that are labelled like this: C/B♭, E/G♯. What's going on here, exactly?

**A:** In short, the chords you mention are called 'slash chords' – not the prettiest name, but functionally descriptive, at least.

When you see a chord symbol like C/B♭ it means that it's a normal C major chord but with a B♭ in the bass, which has the effect of changing the sound of the chord quite significantly. Similarly an E/G♯ chord would be an E major chord with a G♯ in the bass.

So slash chords are really information for the bass player – you could carry on playing a straight C major, but the bass player would know to play a B♭ under it.

If you're playing the song solo, you would have to adapt the chord shape to include the bass note – but ignoring it is another option. It wouldn't be wrong – the chord is still fundamentally a C major – but it wouldn't be quite 'right' at the same time.

**Q:** Could you tell me why some 7th chords are called 'dominants'? Seems a bit of an odd name and conjures up visions of leather-clad chords beating the rest of the scale tones into submission! Surely the key note of the scale is the most dominant in nature?

**A:** The quick answer is that the use of the word 'dominant' is one of music's anachronisms from the days when each note of the scale had a name rather than a number to denote its position. If you check out the diagram below, you'll see all the original names of the notes from yesteryear:

You probably already know that the dominant 7th chord in any key is built upon its fifth note – a.k.a. the 'dominant' – and that its main job is to lead the ear back to the tonic, as in the progression below:

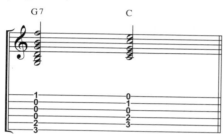

It's the only chord in any key that can do this particular job well and the reason why it has hung on to its older identity is probably to distinguish it from the other types of 7th that abound in music – major 7ths, diminished 7ths and so on.

Fear not, it's nothing to do with music theory straying into top shelf magazine territory!

**Q:** I heard a couple of guys at a gig recently talking about the Robben Ford pentatonic scale – I didn't know Robben had his own scale! Could you tell me what it is, please?

**A:** In interviews and on his excellent tuition videos Robben says that he uses a custom version of the blues pentatonic scale which includes the 6th – a note not usually resident in the good old-fashioned minor pentatonic. This has the effect of 'sweetening up' the scale a little whilst making it sound a bit jazzy, too. If you check out the music example below you will be able to see that by adding this one note, you can bring the blues scale one step closer to a Dorian mode – a favourite of jazz players and renowned for its sweet'n'sour characteristics.

**Q:** Could you please explain what 'palm muting' is? I keep seeing it referred to in books, but I don't know what it is.

**A:** When playing some rhythm or lead parts, it's sometimes necessary to try and restrain the guitar's natural tendency to 'ring on' once a string or collection of strings has been sounded. This is where the edge of the right-hand palm comes in, er, handy; if you lightly rest the 'karate chop' edge of the picking hand on the strings near the bridge it has the effect of muting the strings slightly and hence controls the sustain.

Try this simple experiment: rest your palm's edge lightly in front of the bridge and play the open strings. The pressure with your palm should be just enough to let the strings ring, but not enough to mute them completely. Now experiment with the pressure of your hand so that you hear everything from ringing strings to a dull thud. These are the parameters that you'll work between when using palm muting; sometimes you'll just want to take the edge off a ringing chord and sometimes you'll want to cut it dead. As with everything technique related on the guitar, this will take a bit of practice, but I'm sure you'll get there very soon!

**Q:** I've been playing guitar for a few years now, but having recently bought a metronome I'm working on trying to increase my speed. My self-taught picking style is a combination of alternate picking and economy picking. I was wondering whether I should overhaul my technique by using strict alternate picking in order to improve my speed?

**A:** There is a considerable amount of controversy about picking in guitar teaching circles. I know there are some who champion economy picking and there are those who valiantly defend alternate picking as the only true faith. There are even some who have managed to achieve impressive results using a home-grown hybrid – so where to start?

Personally, I believe that alternate picking is easily the most durable in nearly all styles as you never have to adapt scale fingerings on the fretboard to suit a picking regime as you do with some methods, and so I would recommend that this is where you start with your metronome. Don't be too ambitious, though; start out at a very slow pace because it will take time for your hands, eyes and brain to adjust to the new discipline. Don't forget that agility on the fretboard can also be down to solid left-hand legato techniques and so you might want to do some work in this area, too.

**Q:** Where's middle C on my guitar? I read something about it being in a different place to other instruments but I don't see how this can be so. Isn't there some sort of internationally agreed standard for middle C?

**A:** I must say that I love the idea of their being an international watchdog that convenes in order to to iron out irregularities in music theory's nightmarish world!

It's not that the actual pitch of middle C is different on the guitar – you'll find that the first fret on the B string agrees in pitch with a piano or any other instrument for that matter. The confusion comes in when music is written down for the guitar as we 'read' middle C as being an octave below on the third fret, A string. If you look at the diagram, you'll understand why we do this; if we notated middle C at its true pitch location, we'd be well and truly onto the bass clef by the time we got down to the notes on the D string, something that would make reading for the guitar even more awkward than it is already. So guitar music is 'transposed' by an octave so that everyday guitar music can sit on a single clef. In other words, your notated middle C will sound an octave lower than a piano, but it's only in music's paperwork that this anomaly occurs.

Middle C's actual pitch on the guitar is found here…

…but we read it here…

…otherwise your bass E string would end up way down here on the bass clef!

**Q:** Is there a right and a wrong way to hold a plectrum if you want to do some fairly nifty lead playing? Everyone seems to hold their pick differently and claims theirs to be the only way!

**A:** There is a variety of ways to hold that simple lump of plastic and most of them work just fine. I've seen plenty of oddball examples of plectrum etiquette in my time: jazz maestro Joe Pass used to break his picks in half so that they were really small, Buddy Guy uses huge great kite-shaped objects, Robben Ford uses the 'blunt' end of his pick to strike the strings, claiming it gives a fatter sound, Eddie Van Halen holds his between thumb and middle finger – the list is endless. The point is that they all work for the individual concerned but probably not on a wider scale. Certainly, the default method is to grasp the pick between finger and thumb and strike the string using about the top 2mm – don't grip too hard as this creates tension in the hand and don't form the remaining fingers into a fist as this will tense up muscles unnecessarily, too. The rest, as they say, is up to you!

**Q:** Can you tell me what the difference is between a major 7th and a dominant 7th, please? I'm not sure which one to use.

**A:** Quite simply, the difference is that they belong to totally different scales. Take a look at the diagram below: the major 7th belongs to the major scale and if we form a chord using the root, 3rd, 5th and 7th, it results in a major 7th.

If we do exactly the same trick with the dominant scale (or Mixolydian mode if you prefer) using exactly the same formula, it results in a dominant 7th. Technically speaking, these two scales imply different keys; C major would obviously be in C, but C7 would actually be in the key of F or F minor. If you play the two scales one after the other you can see that there is an immediate difference and this is passed on to the chords, too.

So it's very important to use the correct one called for each time as playing the wrong one will sound ghastly.

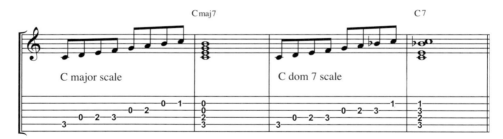

**Q:** At a band practice recently I came across an Em7♭5 chord and couldn't remember how to play it. The keyboard player, who has music lessons after school, said I could play C9 instead because it was almost the same chord. I tried it and it seemed to fit in OK but this can't be right, surely? I know the keyboard player is a smartass smug git, but this sounds like voodoo to me!

**A:** Much as I share your reservations about keyboard players, I've got to say that

he was right in this case. The problem is that we've only got 12 notes to share between literally thousands of chords and so it's not surprising that we tend to duplicate them quite often.

This is known as 'chord substitution' in cloistered jazz circles, where a chord can be swapped for one with a similar array of notes in it to good effect. I know it's confusing, but take a look at the diagram on the next page and you'll see how Em7b5 and C9 are just about a perfect match.

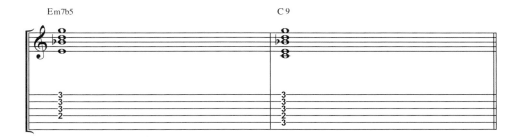

## Q: How do chords get their names?

**A:** Once upon a time, chords didn't exist because man hadn't invented an instrument that could effectively play more than one note at a time. Even the human voice wasn't harmonised in the way we know it today – music wasn't written down and so it was very difficult to get people to reproduce anything the same way twice. Most of the population couldn't read or write in any case and so learning to notate music was realistically placed on the back burner. In the end it was up to the church to start recording music by writing it down. The scribes – monks and friars – started to formulate a way to write music, but things were still very basic. To put it simply, music was in a bit of a mess.

By the time the Renaissance came along things began to improve. A system of notation had been streamlined, instruments like the lute and harpsichord were on the scene and blissful harmony became possible at last. Music grew up a lot around this time and the ensuing baroque era managed to put a lot of the finishing touches to the whole business. We moved away from modality, started to agree on how instruments should be tuned – you've possibly heard of 'just intonation' where all the intervals of the scale are mathematically the same distance apart – and some sort of harmony became possible.

Obviously I'm skipping over a few hundred years quite quickly here, but I thought a thumbnail sketch of music's past was necessary before we come up to date.

In any case, harmony – and the naming of chords – begins with the scale. For convenience, I'll use the major scale that we're all familiar with, but this system that I'm about to explain forms the basis for how all scales are harmonised.

First, let's look at the C major scale:

You've seen and heard it before – the major scale is the most common in music. So how exactly do we begin to form chords? Well, way back in the early days of harmony, it was decided that major and minor 3rds would form the basis for chord formation. Don't ask me why it was the 3rd they picked upon – it could have easily been a 4th and music would have sounded very different. But they decided on the 3rd. These particular critters sound like this:

Once again, you've heard both the major and minor variations before, without doubt. To put it very simply, the architects of harmony took a major scale and piled thirds on top of each other. This has the effect of using every other note in the scale – use one, miss one, like this:

G
E
C D E F G A B C

To build that particular pile, I took the note C, missed out the next scale note (D) and used E. Then I missed out the F and used the G to give us a harmonised C note and a chord called C major. It's called a major chord because it has a major 3rd in the middle – an interval that is exactly five frets or semitones long. In order to keep things symmetrical we can now use exactly the same ploy for the other notes of the scale.

| G | A | B | C | D | E | F | G |
|---|---|---|---|---|---|---|---|
| E | F | G | A | B | C | D | E |
| C | D | E | F | G | A | B | C |
| 1 | 2 | 3 | 4 | 5 | 6 | 7 | 1 |

Or, to put things in more familiar surroundings:

So now, let's sort out which chords have a major 3rd in the middle – making them major chords – and which have minor thirds (four frets long) in the middle – making them minor chords.

CEG = C major
DFA = D minor
EGB = E minor
FAC = F major
GBD = G major
ACE = A minor
BDF = Oh, dear...

On the last note of the scale things go horribly wrong. We've got a minor 3rd in the middle, which makes it minor in essence, but then another minor 3rd on top, which means it's not like the others at all. All the others have either a major 3rd with a minor 3rd on top of it, like this:

C – E = major 3rd
E – G = minor 3rd

Or the other way around:

D – F = minor 3rd
F – A = major 3rd

Which means that the root of the chord is the same distance from the second 3rd along the chromatic scale – music's master scale:

C – G = seven semitones
D – F = seven semitones

But when we get to the B:

B – D = minor 3rd
D – F = minor 3rd

So the distance from the B to the F is one semitone short – or 'diminished'. In the end, it doesn't matter because despite this foreshortening, the chord of B 'diminished' actually sounds 'right' when played in context with the other chords in the scale.

With this system of stacking 3rds in place, it means that we can carry on adding another layer to turn all the chords we have so far into some kind of 7th:

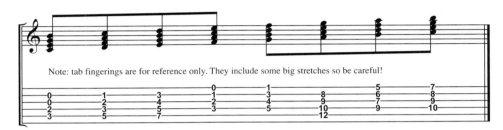

Note: tab fingerings are for reference only. They include some big stretches so be careful!

| B | C | D | E | F | G | A | B |
|---|---|---|---|---|---|---|---|
| G | A | B | C | D | E | F | G |
| E | F | G | A | B | C | D | E |
| C | D | E | F | G | A | B | C |
| 1 | 2 | 3 | 4 | 5 | 6 | 7 | 1 |

This now gives us these chords:

CEGB = C major 7
DFAC = D minor 7
EGBD = E minor 7
FACE = F major 7
GBDF = G7
ACEG = A minor 7
BDFA = Oh, not again...

Two things have happened: the G major chord has been transformed to its more familiar guise of the dominant 7th and that troublesome B chord has caused problems again. We can deal with the B chord by renaming it – basically a diminished chord with a 7th on top is called a 'minor 7th, flat 5th' and is abbreviated thus:

Bm7♭5

But what's happened to the G? Here the chord formula reads like this – a three-note major chord (or 'triad') with a minor 3rd on top becomes a dominant chord – and there's only one of these per major scale.

So, very basically, if you find yourself with a group of notes and you're unsure what to call them, first of all check out the key the piece is in. Usually it's fairly easy to tell if a song is in A or G or D – if you're not sure, the key is usually the last chord played in the piece (this isn't always the case, but most of the time it's true).

Then, think about the harmonised scale in that key – even if you have to write it down. Then think about what the chords would be in that key – they'll always be in the same order:

**Major, Minor, Minor, Major, Seventh, Minor, Diminished**

It's quite likely that this is as far as you'll have to go – you'll find some sort of a match this way around and you'll have a name for your chord. If not, you'll have to do some more detective work. Is the group of notes you're looking to name similar to one of the chords from the harmonised scale? Is it some kind of extended chord like a 9th or 11th? Has the song changed key in the middle? Things like that. Obviously this is a very vast subject and books on harmony are notoriously thick as a house brick, but might be your only option, should you want to investigate further.

## Q: How do I know which scale fits over any particular chord?

**A:** I'll try to be gentle, but the fact is that asking a question as apparently straightforward as 'which scale fits over this chord?' means that you're beginning to delve into the realm of music mechanics – literally how music works and why – and this relies on learning some theory. I've never thought that this is too unreasonable – after all, you need at least an appreciation of how a car works before you can expect to do a good job servicing or maintaining it.

The second point I'd like to make – and I apologise for hopping onto my soapbox for a minute here – is that I'm not personally a fan of people learning to play by using the 'chord/scale' slide rule technique. It's too scientific to be much of a true aid to the creative process – and learning that such-and-such a scale fits over 'chord x' is really only learning half the story.

This kind of thinking is fine for the purposes of research in the classroom, but it really needs to stay there and not be taken forward onto the bandstand and 'applied' in a cold, mathematical way. The results are rarely musically valid, although it is possible to impress a certain sector of the audience with your apparent speed and fluency. But followers of this system of learning always fall over when they're asked to play a slow, sensitive ballad, because it exposes the area that can't be covered by pure music science – playing melodically. So please don't

mistake this kind of thinking for a viable 'method'; use it instead to audition material in the practice room and to train your fingers. Listen to the effect a scale has when played over a chord and file the sound away in your brain. When you need to reproduce its unique sonic characteristic in a solo or improvisation, it will be there waiting.

Right, let's take a C major triad and see what kind of noise we can make over it. We've seen that this particular chord comprises the following notes:

**C Maj = C E G**

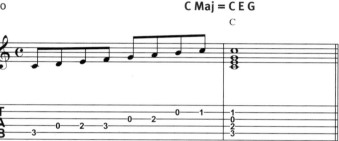

Usually, the first thing we'd suspect is that this chord would take an ordinary major scale over the top and everything would, indeed, sound dandy as a result.

We saw earlier in this chapter how the thinking behind this chord/scale partnership works – how a triad can be extracted from a scale and so on. But the truth of the matter is that this triad can support any scale that has the same root, third and fifth. So, as an example, let's look at the scale of C Lydian:

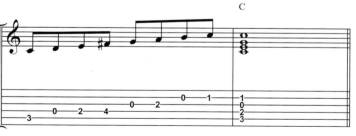

You'll notice here how the notes of the scale are thus:

| C | D | E | F♯ | G | A | B | C |
|---|---|---|----|---|---|---|---|
| 1 | 2 | 3 | ♯4 | 5 | 6 | 7 | 1 |

There's an F♯ in there – a sharpened 4th – instead of the regular F natural seen in the Ionian or major scale and it's this diversion which gives the Lydian its unique sound signature. But the important thing to notice is that the two scales share the same triad.

Major:   C D E F G A B C
         1 2 3 4 5 6 7 1
Triad:   C E G
         1 3 5

Lydian:  C D E F♯ G A B C
         1 2 3 ♯4 5 6 7 1
Triad:   C E G
         1 3 5

In this way, we can say that there's not just one scale that would be a prime candidate for use in improvisation over this chord, there are at least two.

Let's take another example; this time we'll take a basic minor chord:

C minor: C E♭ G
         1 ♭3 5

Once again, the obvious choice for a scale to improvise with would be the straightforward Aeolian, known to its friends as the natural minor:

Now this scale looks like this on paper:

| C | D | E♭ | F | G | A♭ | B♭ | C |
|---|---|-----|---|---|-----|-----|---|
| 1 | 2 | ♭3  | 4 | 5 | ♭6  | ♭7  | 1 |

But it shares its triad with at least one other scale – look at the Dorian:

The Dorian scale contains these intervals:

| C | D | E♭ | F | G | A | B♭ | C |
|---|---|-----|---|---|---|-----|---|
| 1 | 2 | ♭3  | 4 | 5 | 6 | ♭7  | 1 |

And when we check out the triad:

C E♭ G
1 ♭3 5

We can see that, once again, the shoe fits and so the Dorian scale would be a plausible vehicle to use in order to improvise over a C minor chord.

And, what about the guitarist's favourite scale – the minor pentatonic?

49

C min pentatonic: **C E♭ F G B♭**

This scale can be looked on as a 'reduced' form of the full minor scale, but one glance will tell you that the triad information is still present in there and so this scale would work over an ordinary C minor, too.

The whole subject of scale/chord synonyms is thrown wide open when we begin to consider the dominant chord family. The Mixolydian is, of course, the perfect fit for a basic 7th chord:

C7:          **C E G B♭**
             **1 3 5 ♭7**

C Mixolydian:  **C D E F G A B♭ C**
               **1 2 3 4 5 6 ♭7 1**

This time we're not necessarily considering just a triad – we've got to acknowledge the fact that the dominant chord family derives much of its power musically speaking from the relationship between the 3rd and flat 7th

forming the dissonant flat 5th sound:

$$E - B♭ = ♭5th$$

So this time we're really looking for scales that fit in with the four note formula for the dominant chord. One fairly obvious candidate is the major pentatonic:

C major pentatonic:     **C D E G A**

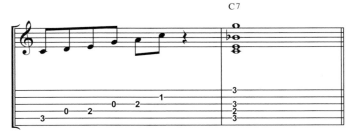

The basic triad is still in there, but, by avoiding the dominant 7th altogether, it's still a good fit.

Jazz and fusion players thrive on altered dominant sounds and here there are many chord and scale relationships to consider.

We could sharpen the fourth of the chord, for instance, and get a slightly 'outside' sound.

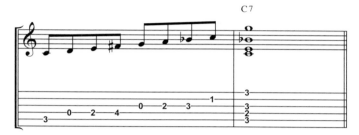

C Lydian dominant: **C D E F♯ G A Bb C**
**1 2 3 ♯4 5 6 b7 1**

The point is that the basic dominant chord is still intact.

Naturally, we're only really taking a brief peek into the wild and whacky world of chord and scale relationships here, but these principles remain pretty much uncorrupted all the way through. It's worth noting that no amount of Thesaurus type knowledge where scales are concerned is a substitute for having a developed sense of context. In other words, it's possible to squeeze all sorts of scales into a single improvisation, but if it ends up sounding either too far 'out there' or just plain wrong, then what's the point?

If I can make one final plea it is for you to remember that the job's not done when this lesson is learned. A scale is to music like the alphabet is to literature; there are still a couple of creative blanks to fill in before the process is complete!

**Q:** What is a G5 chord? G normally has a 5th in it so why specify it?

**A:** A '5 chord' is so called because it actually omits the third. Back in the sixties and seventies players discovered that chords containing thirds could sound harmonically very confused through a distorted amp, but chords without this interval sounded truly riffmungous! Today's amp technology means that fuller chords can still sound great through high gain settings,

but we still fall back on the good old rock'n'roll staple of 5th chords every so often and so the distinction is made in the chord name so a 5th chord isn't confused with an ordinary major.

**Q:** Is there a quick way to remember key signatures? I'm studying music for GCSE and can never remember how many sharps or flats there are in the various keys.

**A:** Various ways have been suggested to me in the past, but I've never really found one that was instantly memorable. Some people tie key signatures in with the cycle of fourths and remember that the flat keys increase one flat at a time when you go clockwise and then, at the bottom of the chart the sharp keys take over and diminish by one sharp at a time until you reach C at the top, which has neither sharps nor flats in its key signature. Maybe if you copied out the cycle of fourths on a large piece of paper and hung it on your wall for a while you'd find you slowly pick them up just by familiarity.

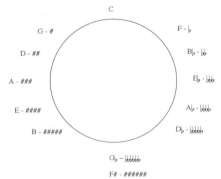

**Q:** My parents have offered to buy me some lessons as a 12th birthday present, but when they phoned a local teacher they were told that if I learned piano first I would find the guitar a lot easier. I can't see that this is right, could you shed any light on the subject, please?

**A:** It sounds to me like this particular teacher doesn't really want to teach you guitar at all and is on some kind of campaign to teach you keyboards no matter what! Speaking as someone who spent a couple of years unwillingly having piano lessons when I was young, I can say for certain that the disciplines of the two instruments are almost entirely different. In fact I can't think of a single advantage to learning piano before the guitar...

My advice would be to draw your parents' attention to the Registry of Guitar Tutors website at www.registryofguitartutors.com and seek their advice. They offer graded exams and have a list of tutors in every area.

**Q:** I was told by a teacher that the way to learn to use the modes is to remember that they're all a major scale, shifted by a certain number of scale tones. For instance, if you want a D Dorian scale, you think of the major scale a tone lower than the root and so on. This sounds very complex to me, though – what do you think?

**A:** Personally, I think that way too much emphasis is placed on the modes. The popular thought seems to be that they are some sort of shortcut to effective melodic soloing and this is simply not the case. There's no doubt that the modes actually permeate modern guitar music and learning them forms an important part of the overall 'package', so to speak. But they will only ever reach their full potential as a soloing tool if the sounds of the individual modes are in your head – and this is where a little work in the area of ear training will pay off. By all means play through each mode as part of your practice routine, but instead of using a slide rule and a set of compasses to find them, listen to how they sound. You'll find that some sound better than others to you and that you'll slowly absorb the information of where to locate them naturally and will eventually be able to call on them intuitively. Having to work out where a particular mode is using some form of advanced music maths is insane, as far as I'm concerned!

**Q:** I've been playing blues for some time and I notice that the 7♯9 chord crops up a lot of the time, but it's the only 'altered' chord to do so. Why does this particular chord fit so well in a blues?

**A:** I wouldn't say it's the only altered seventh chord in blues – certainly not if we talk about a player like Robben Ford, for example. Arguably, the diminished chord is a form of altered seventh and that crops up in blues fairly frequently, too. But, if you want my own opinion as to why the 7♯9 (or the 'Hendrix chord' as we used to call it) makes such an ideal blues chord, we've really only got to look at its innards...

Most seventh chords are based around this chord formula:

C7:     C E G B♭
        1 3 5 ♭7

The 7♯9, in its most usual guitar voicing, looks like this:

C7♯9:   C E B♭ D♯
        1 3 ♭7 ♯9

Now technically speaking this chord actually gets its dissonant character from the clash between the 3rd and sharp 9th – literally, we're cramming both the minor and major 3rds into the same chord and so there's two semitones clashing against one another. This kind of thing is uncommon in music – we generally have either the major or minor 3rd present but not both. But having both together here outlines something that happens in blues anyway – that is, the 'blue minor 3rd' which slightly sharp in pitch and gives us that lovely bluesy wail in many blues licks. It's not strictly major or minor, but a kind of fusion between both. So, the 7♯9 chord actually mimics this, providing us with a harmonised version of the blues' basic restless sound.

**Q:** Should I concentrate on learning pieces, scales, or trying to build my technique with exercises?

**A:** You should do all the things you suggest and you'll find that you can do so quite successfully as long as you manage your time well. When you sit down to practise, begin with some simple warm-up and gentle stretching exercises. Then focus on practising some scales with a metronome to gain some coordination skills. Gradually increase the speed of the metronome over a period of time and be very strict with yourself as far as accuracy is concerned.

Don't be content to move on to another notch on the metronome until all the notes are ringing clear – I recommend that you practise without distortion or even acoustically so that you can keep a strict ear open in the interests of quality control. Then move on to 'work in progress' – this could entail learning a new song or solo. Finally, have some fun; put on a backing track and wail away, or whatever takes your fancy. If you work within strictly controlled sections like this you'll make progress smoothly and surely.

**Q:** After watching various DVDs I noticed some players play with the thumb hidden behind the fretboard whereas others have the thumb poking above or just hooking over the top of the fretboard. I once was told by a hardened classical player that the thumb should be kept straight at all times. So, what effect does the thumb position/placement have and what should be the guide for the thumb for different types of playing for maximum performance and ease of playing? Also, is it possible to damage your hand/muscles/tendons by playing with a bad technique or too much, or too hard/stretchy too soon?

**A:** Thumb position on the guitar is critical in that it has to do the job of acting as a counterweight for the fingers. If the thumb is allowed to wander too far from the vertical – to the left or right at the back of the neck – it will be difficult for the fingers to apply the correct pressure to fret notes and chords successfully.

As far as actual positioning is concerned, it really depends on how high you wear the guitar. Classical players have a very disciplined playing position with the nut of the guitar level with the left shoulder which makes the 'thumb at the back of the neck' rule correct in order to facilitate fingering. But electric guitarists tend to play with a far more 'low slung' attitude and so the classical thumb position is entirely inappropriate.

So the rule is to keep your thumb as straight as possible and to make sure that it is providing the correct opposite force for the fingers at all times.

You're right about poor technique giving rise to medical problems, too; in a lot of cases conditions like tendonitis can be avoided by paying attention to playing stance and by reducing tension in hands, wrists and forearms to the absolute minimum (see the chapter on Medical Matters for more on muscles and tendons).

**Q:** I recently mastered the art of playing natural harmonics on my electric but someone told me that you can play 'artificial harmonics', too. Could you tell me what they are and how to play them?

**A:** The strongest harmonic can be found exactly 12 frets higher than a note. For instance, when you play the harmonic at the 12th fret on your top E string, you are hearing another E note an octave higher.

So the theory is that this remains possible for every note, all we have to do is to find a method for playing it. So, if you play the F♯ at the second fret on your top E and count 12 frets up, you'll reach the F♯ at the 14th fret. If you stop the string with your right-hand index finger and use one of the other fingers on that hand to pluck the string, you'll find the harmonic.

It takes a bit of practice, but with a little bit of patience, you'll soon be playing artificial harmonics all over the neck.

**Q:** I read somewhere about an interval called a tenth, but I can't find a definition – it's not in any of my guitar books. What's going on?

**A:** This is something that makes more sense to a keyboard player, rather than a guitarist. A tenth is a third an octave up from the root (see diagram) and so, if we wanted a tenth along the C scale, it would work out like this:

| C | D | E | F | G | A | B | C | D | E |
|---|---|---|---|---|---|---|---|---|---|
| 1 | 2 | 3 | 4 | 5 | 6 | 7 | 1 | 9 | 10 |

Usually, in most guitar books at any rate, this interval is still referred to as a third, but keyboard players know it as a natty accompaniment device.

If you're ever in doubt about the intervals in the upper reaches, just subtract seven from them to identify their true position in the scale.

For instance, if we take a ninth, we do the maths like this:

$$9 - 7 = 2$$

And, of course, a ninth is just the second degree of the scale an octave up.

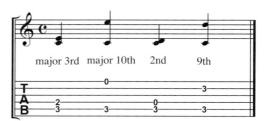

**Q:** Which techniques can be used on an acoustic guitar to substitute for those exciting and emotional whole step bends whereby you can still wring out the same emotion and excitement? And more specifically, if you were to play an electric lead piece that you already know on acoustic and it contains 4th into 5th and ♭7th into root bends, for example, what might you do in its place? Would you have to re-phrase the figure?

**A:** You're certainly right in thinking that bending strings is far more difficult on acoustic than it is on electric! Heavy gauge strings take an enormous amount of 'push' by comparison and anything more than a half step bend seems like an Olympian feat.

So, many players substitute slides for bends which means that the pitches of bent notes can be reproduced without too much effort.

If you want to transfer your electric style over to acoustic, you will have to rethink many of your licks to incorporate slides – keep the notes the same, just alter the way in which you play them.

**Q:** I'm a little confused about minor scales (although I'm OK with the minor pentatonic). There seems to be so many different ones and no one can tell me which are the best ones to learn and in which order or anything. Can you help?

**A:** From an ear training point of view, I think it's best to familiarise yourself first of all with the natural minor scale as arguably this is the most common version of the minor you will use. If you concentrate all your efforts on learning this scale all over the fretboard, your ear will become accustomed to its sound and then you will be primed to introduce it to all of the the variations. Next

in line, I would say the Dorian is a good one to work at as it's a minor 7th scale, essentially, and heard quite often as a variation in blues playing by some of the more adventurous artists out there.

After this, I would suggest that you look at the harmonic and melodic minors and then begin to explore the other modal minors like the Phrygian and Locrian (see example). Then, feel free to explore some of the modes of the minor scales.

There is a lot of work here, but it's important that you take your time over this as your ear needs to absorb all of the different nuances inherent in the various minor scales.

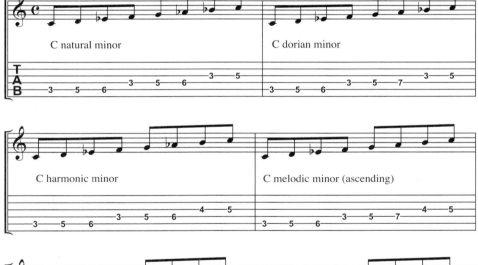

**Q:** Can pick thickness, size, material, etc have an effect on a player's style or sound? I borrowed a pick from a friend and somehow it seemed easier to play some stuff – and it sounded better, too! What's going on?

**A:** Anything that touches the strings can have an effect on the tone you produce and so, in general, pick thickness and material can make a considerable difference, whereas actual physical size can just be down to personal taste.

The most obvious example of this is the difference in tone produced by alternating between a thin plastic pick and a thicker one: the flexibility of a thin pick – that's anything around .44mm–.78mm – would suit acoustic strumming and offer a brightish tone at the same time – but they tend not to be as good for lead playing.

The thicker variety – say, 1mm and beyond – tend to help precision, which is good news for fast single note picking. Thick picks help introduce dynamics into your playing, too, because they don't flex as much and lose you some 'whack' by absorbing impact. In general the tone from the heavyweights tends to be more rounded and mellow, too – although some metal picks would be the exception to this rule.

Next time you pay a visit to the local music store, invest in a few picks of different weights and sizes (it will be the cheapest investment in your playing that you've ever made!) and audition them – you'll probably find one that suits you.

**Q:** I haven't been playing very long and I'm having serious problems with my vibrato. My friend says that it sounds like someone's trodden on the cat's tail – is there a knack to it or something I'm missing?

**A:** Vibrato takes everyone time to master, so be patient. Most beginners find that they are being too frantic with the left hand which leads to an unfocused and uneven vibrato instead of a single continuous, flowing movement.

The correct method is actually quite subtle; you need to concentrate on wrist action – a gentle 'shake' is all that's needed – and make sure that all the energy generated from the wrist is brought down to the finger and into the string. Try it very slowly and listen hard to the sound you make – don't 'over-bend' the string as you move it as good vibrato begins with only a minor variation in pitch. Keep practising it every day and you will soon hear an improvement.

**Q:** I would be very grateful for some advice on picking. I am aware of the debate between alternate and economy picking and am finding that my deliberation on the style of picking to use is holding me back. When practising licks or a solo I want to use the same type of picking each time I play each section in order to get them under my fingers but am never sure whether to approach it from an economy or alternate picking point of view.

**A:** To begin with, let's try to define the two basic picking techniques: alternate picking is the strict up and down movement of the pick on all scale or melodic passages and many players swear by this method as being the most adaptable (we'll talk about exactly how it's adapted in a minute).

Economy picking comes into its own when a passage calls for a change of strings (see example). Here, the pick 'follows through' to the next string which means two consecutive down strokes when moving from bass to treble and two consecutive up strokes when going in the opposite direction.

The actual 'economy' is gained from not having to move the pick over the string to produce an upstroke on a string change –

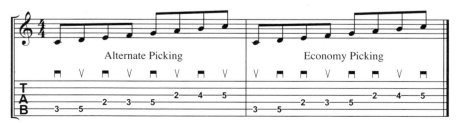

and followers of this technique insist that it increases fluency and speed.

Alternate picking is a discipline that will train the right hand to a high standard, but doesn't really take into account the fact that many passages are slurred – or played legato, if you prefer – meaning that the left hand becomes responsible for generating its fair share of notes, too.

Even the most devout disciples of alternate picking will agree that there are times where the dynamics of the piece they are playing are best expressed by using consecutive down strokes (some riff passages, for instance). So, despite the apparent rigidness of alternate picking, it is more generally adapted to suit the music at hand.

Economy picking can, of course, be adapted in a similar fashion but, like alternate picking, has to be 'programmed in' to the hands by practising scales continually for some time first.

I must admit that I advocate alternate picking as I believe it to be the most practical – but that's not to say that I pick every note strictly up and down. My only concern with economy picking is where scale patterns or shapes on the fretboard have to be altered so that there is always the necessary 'follow through' between strings.

I watched a video once which featured a very well-known player who recommended that the flat 2nd was included in the major scale and played on the bass string 'to make the numbers work' and guarantee the consecutive ups and downs be positioned correctly. This is, of course, nonsense as the flat second has no place in the major scale whatsoever. This type of distortion of music theory is, I'm afraid, where my sympathies with economy picking end!

My recommendation is to follow your own path where picking is concerned and don't allow yourself to be swayed by anyone. Experiment with both disciplines and you're sure to find one that fits your style.

**Q:** What finger do you use for tapping? I use my ring finger so that I can keep my plectrum in a normal position between forefinger and thumb, but people tell me I'm weird and the correct way to do it is to put the pick somewhere (in my mouth) and use my index or middle fingers. Now I know how to take criticism, but surely if my way works it's OK?

**A:** Don't worry, you're not weird... There are no rules as to which finger – or indeed fingers – you should use to tap. There are plenty of players out there who use combinations of fingers that are unique to them and they all make them work. Jennifer Batten and Guthrie Govan use all four fingers of the right hand to tap, with epic results. Check out Jennifer's version of 'The Flight Of The Bumble Bee' and you'll see what I mean.

Basically, a lot of the techniques associated with modern day guitar playing are down to the rule of 'whatever feels right' to the player – there is no Highway Code for this sort of thing, let me assure you!

**Q:** I've been reading about 'drop 2' and 'drop 3' chords in some jazz books. What are they and how easy are they to play?

**A:** I must admit that this was a new term to me. I have my suspicions that it's another new music term that has been imported from certain music colleges where jazz is taught like geography and even the simplest piece of music mechanics is enthusiastically complicated by giving it a fancy name...

After a little research, I managed to find that 'drop 2 and drop 3' chords are really nothing more than inversions used in the process of harmonising a melody. It's a pretty heady concept, so hang on to your hat.

If you want to produce an instrumental version of a song to play on the guitar, it's likely that you'll start with a fake book or 'lead sheet' where all you are given is the melody and chord symbols for a song. In order to come up with something that sounds 'whole' on the guitar it's necessary to juggle with the chords to a certain extent so that the melody remains clear on top of the accompaniment. In some cases, you have to invert some of the chords (see example below) especially if the melody note in question is also a chord tone. Obviously it's important that the melody is clearly defined in these instances and not 'lost' within the chord itself.

A drop 2 chord is where the second note below the melody is dropped to the bass in order to get it out of the melody's way. A drop 3 chord is the same sort of idea, but involves the third note away from the melody.

I've come up with a couple of examples that I hope illustrate how these things work – like I say, I hadn't heard of the terms, but it's something I do all the time if I'm arranging a chord melody tune – I just wasn't aware that someone had given it a name!

**Q:** I've just about mastered the pentatonic scale in all positions on the fretboard, but I don't know which scale I should start practising next. I play mainly rock with a little bit of modern pop every so often.

**A:** You don't mention if your mastery of the pentatonic scale includes both major and minor versions. If not, then this is something that definitely needs attention. At the same time it would be worth checking out the ordinary major scale in all five positions, too. Despite chatter in internet forums about the relevance of modes and the various minor scales, the major scale is

by far the most widely used in western music. Only by fully understanding this particular scale from both aural and fretboard points of view can you hope to extend your vocabulary into more exotic scale forms later on.

There are a few books on the market that will show you 'maps' of all of the scales on the guitar neck and one of these would certainly be a wise investment!

**Q:** I've being trying to learn some theory recently and have come across something I just don't understand. How does a diminished seventh chord get its name? If my understanding is correct it doesn't actually contain a seventh at all and so how come it's known as a 'diminished seventh'?

**A:** The way that a diminished seventh gets its name is like this: the basic diminished triad exists within the harmonised scale (see the example on page 46) on the seventh degree. In the key of C, this would be B diminished and would include the notes B, D and F.

If we analyse the relationship between these notes, we find that B is the root, D is the flat 3rd and F is the flat 5th. So both of these important triad members – the 3rd and 5th – have been dropped by a semitone. In other words, they have been 'diminished' by one semitone each. 'Diminished' is just an old fashioned music term for 'reduced' or 'lessened'.

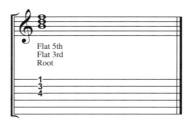

Now, you probably already know that all of the triads in the harmonised scale can be turned into 7ths by adding another 3rd on top. In this way, C major becomes C major 7th, D minor becomes D minor 7th and so on. When we get to the B, we add another 3rd and find ourselves with A and so the B chord now spells B D F A, which makes a minor seven, flat five or m7♭5 for short. This chord is also sometimes known as the 'half diminished' as two of its notes have been dropped by a semitone, but the root and 7th are still musically 'intact'.

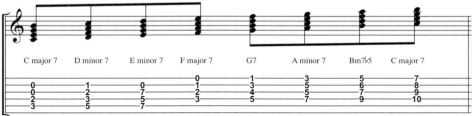

*Warning: big stretches in TAB – for illustration only

The full diminished 7th comes about when we drop the 7th a semitone as well. So, in this case, the A becomes A♭ – literally a 'diminished' 7th.

So the formula for a diminished 7th is root, flat third, flat fifth and flat dominant 7th (sometimes called a 'double flat' 7th).

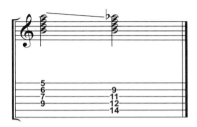

**Q:** The problem is my picking hand. When it comes to speed picking single notes repeatedly I can hold it for a little while but then my elbow sort of takes over when my wrist gives up and I can't seem to stop it from doing so. My hands don't co-ordinate properly either...

**A:** You need to strip this area of your playing right down and spend some time looking at every part of it closely. I usually recommend that students imagine that a part of their playing machine isn't working correctly and it needs to spend some time on the workbench to get it functioning properly again.

First of all, impose a speed limit on your playing while you work on it – don't even attempt to play anything fast because you'll just find the problem recurring and that won't get you anywhere. Begin with some simple single string exercises and play them slowly, taking a good look at what's happening with both arms while you do. Don't be tempted to speed up, just take things really slow at a comfortable metronome setting.

Aim to spend at least a week on 'slow' before moving the metronome speed up a couple of notches at a time. At every point, keep a check on what's happening with your hands – my guess is that as you're approaching higher speeds your arms are tensing up. Only time and patience will get you back in the fretboard Grand Prix and so it's worth being very self-disciplined now.

**Q:** Whenever I bend a note on my Epiphone Les Paul it sounds wildly out of tune as I don't know how far to push the string. Is there a way that you can suggest I start training my fingers to bend notes in tune, please?

**A:** I suspect that you haven't been playing for very long, as this is the problem for many beginners when they begin learning how to bend strings. So relax – you're not alone! Bending in tune is a problem we've all encountered at one time or another and it's a thing that solves itself through practice.

If you want a routine to test your bending skills, try this (see diagram): first play the note at the seventh fret on your G string with your third finger, laying fingers one and two on the string behind it. Now, sound your top E string and listen hard to the note it produces. Then try to push the G string up

towards the ceiling until the two notes match. What you're doing here is bending the note D on your third string to the pitch E – a full tone bend.

Try this for a few minutes every day and when you think you're hitting a good in tune E every time, stop sounding the open top string until after the bend to check if you've hit the note at exactly the right pitch.

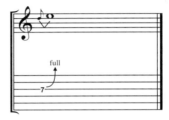

**Q:** I'm still struggling with barre chords after playing for quite a while. I'm obviously doing something wrong – is there a common flaw in this area or should I abandon hope of ever being able to play them?

**A:** It's difficult to know if there's anything wrong with the way you're playing barre chords without being there and actually seeing you attempt one. However, you might like to check a couple of things: are you wearing your strap too low, putting the left hand in a very disadvantageous position to 'grip' the neck satisfactorily?

Or is your playing position bad in general, causing the same sort of problem? Is the action on your guitar too high or the neck dimension simply wrong for you? Are you trying to lay your left-hand index finger down flat? The more correct position is slightly to one side so that the strings contact the finger on the side facing the thumb.

It's likely to be something very simple to put right and I would recommend that you look around for a teacher in your area and book a lesson with him – a good teacher will do

'one off' lessons to address a particular technique and it may only take moments for him to put you back on the right track.

**Q:** I've decided that it's about time that I learned where all the notes are on the fretboard, but I'm struggling. Obviously this is an advantageous thing to know, but it's driving me nuts trying to remember all the time. How does a teacher go about teaching this sort of thing? Is there a fail-safe system or is it just a hard slog?

**A:** We're probably talking hard slog here, I'm afraid. I've found in the past that it's effective to have a student write out a neck chart comprising the first 12 frets of the guitar.

Write only the 'whole notes' on there (i.e. no sharps or flats) so that it doesn't end up looking too crowded and also aim large, too – A3 paper size is just about right. Then put the chart somewhere where you'll see it everyday.

A good ruse for learning at least some of the note positions is to test yourself on either scale roots or moveable chord positions. Every time you sit down to practise, find some chords or scales in different keys – this will make you check where the roots are on your neck chart. Pick different keys at random everyday and you should soon find that you're remembering where more and more notes are located.

**Q:** When I set out to learn chords I thought that the best way to go about it was to buy a chord book and just work through it, but I wasn't prepared for how many chords there are out there – there are thousands! What I need to do is to prioritise the important ones and leave the less important ones until later on, but I don't know which is which – can you provide a list of the order chords ought to be learned in?

**A:** It's healthier to look at a chord book as being more of a dictionary than a workbook. Use it for reference, by all means, but not as a tutor.

Basically, you need to know three different groups of chords: majors, minors and dominant 7ths. These form music's three main chord families and represent a solid way of approaching the building of a chord vocabulary.

Ideally, what you're aiming at is knowing a major, minor and dominant 7th form for each of the 12 notes of the chromatic scale – 36 chords in total. Obviously some of these are harder to play than others and so I introduce players to chords gradually. For instance, I usually start people off on two or three finger chords down at the nut – like E minor, E7, A minor, A7 and so on.

Then I slowly introduce the chords that stretch the left hand like G major, G7 and C major, so that the hand doesn't learn too much too fast, giving it time to adjust to the new activities it's being asked to perform. I try to make sure that chords in the common keys like C, G, D and so on are covered first so

that some simple songs can be tackled as soon as possible meanwhile steering the student towards learning barre chords which opens up the fretboard to all 36 members of the happy strummer's basic repertoire.

**Q:** I'm learning acoustic guitar and have a lot of chords under my fingers, can change between them fairly fast and everything, but it's my right hand that's letting me down. Every time I bash through a song I find myself using the same old repetitive strumming and so everything is beginning to sound samey. I want to try my hand at fingerpicking but I haven't a clue where to start – any chance you can provide a sort of primer?

**A:** The first thing to do is to look at the individual roles of the right-hand fingers and we can do this by practising on open strings.

Very basically, the thumb tends to look after the bass strings – the E, A and D – and the index, middle and ring fingers look after the G, B and E strings respectively. This isn't an exhaustive rule, of course, but it's good enough to get some kind of discipline going in the right hand.

In traditional fingerstyle guitar music, the right-hand fingers are designated letters in order to notate fingering. The thumb is 'p', the index finger is 'i', the middle finger is 'm' and the ring finger is 'a'. Look at the examples I've written out here. To begin with, the thumb plays the open A string whilst the 'i, m and a' fingers play the top three strings.

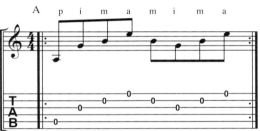

It's unlikely that you'll have long fingernails on your right hand – many fingerstylists develop them so that they have four 'grow-your-own plectrums' to sound the strings, even reinforcing them with nail lacquer to strengthen them if necessary. So for now, you'll probably be playing with the 'meat' of the fingertips.

The other examples I've written out are variations on the basic 'arpeggio' style fingering for the right hand, with a final example on a C major chord to show you how effective this technique can sound when employed as a song accompaniment.

As I say, these are the basics of fingerstyle – there is a lot more to learn and plenty of books, DVDs and so on to learn from – good luck!

**Q:** What's the difference between an augmented chord and an augmented 7th? Surely they're basically the same thing?

**A:** They're certainly not the same thing. Let's look at how basic chords are turned into 7ths in the first place. To begin with, there are four types of triad: major, minor, diminished and augmented (see diagram). These are simple three-note

C dim7                      C aug7

assemblies, one or other of which lay at the heart of virtually every chord in the book.

Anything we add to the basic triad will alter its 'colour' or tone slightly. If we take the major triad and add a 7th (ie the 7th note of the major scale) it becomes a major 7th chord. We can do exactly the same with the minor triad, too; add the 7th note of the minor scale and we have a minor 7th.

Naturally, the same kind of thinking can be applied to the other two triads as well. If we add the appropriate 7th to its triad, we end up with a diminished 7th and the same applies to the augmented.

Compare them both together and I think you'll agree that the augmented and augmented 7th chords have a lot in common, but they're not the same chord by any means.

**Q:** What do you do when your playing gets stuck in a rut? I feel that I've been doing the same old things for ages and every time I try to play a solo, it's always the same sort of thing, just a few licks I've played 1000 times before, strung together willy nilly. I admit that I don't practise as much as I should – but that's mainly because I'm bored with what I'm doing! Please help.

**A:** It sounds like you desperately need some new input to your playing – and some fresh challenges to re-engage your interest. What you're experiencing is known as a 'plateau stage' where nothing seems to be happening and you seem to be getting nowhere. You need to be guided in the right direction and so why not book a few lessons with a teacher? An experienced tutor will have seen this problem before and will know how to push you forward to the next stage in your learning.

**Q:** I've just returned from guitar camp and I noticed that everyone seemed to try and outdo each other with volume when they were meant to be practising or jamming (particularly the younger ones). A thought struck me – do you guys practise at high volume? If so, how do you get away with it? You can't all live in soundproof semis or isolated mansions, surely!

**A:** Speaking personally, I live in a flat and so any thoughts of practising at concert volumes have been permanently shelved in my case! Seriously though, I don't know of anyone who plays at home using the same kind of levels they would use live. Many will practise on an unplugged guitar – you don't need high volume for exercises or scale routines, after all – or use an amp simulator with headphones for private moments of mayhem.

Trying to outdo each other with volume the way you describe is a sign of inexperience or plain uncontrolled youthful exuberance, having had the umbilical of parental control temporarily severed!

**Q:** I realise that this is a naïve question, but how do you improvise a solo? Every time I try I just end up playing some lick I've learned from another solo and it quite often doesn't fit! I want to get into a band but I've really got to get some idea of where improvised solos actually come from.

**A:** Everyone already knows how to improvise – we do it every day of our lives. If I asked you to tell me about your last holiday or a favourite pet you wouldn't be reading from a script, you'd be essentially improvising your reply and it would be different every time you tried it. Just because this type of improvisation involves speech rather than music shouldn't make that much of a difference either. Speech relies on an innate knowledge of language and vocabulary and it's exactly the same with music. We all start with a sort of 'phrase book' capability where we find ourselves limited to repeating something we've memorised – the musical equivalent of asking for directions to the nearest café in a foreign language. The more experienced you become at speaking the foreign language and the more you gain new vocabulary the easier the task of conversation becomes.

If you work on increasing your knowledge of music by keeping a sharp edge on your practice routine you will find that your fluency will gradually increase to the extent that it's your own ideas that form the basis for improvised solos more and more.

**Q:** Someone told me that the most important scale in jazz improvisation is the melodic minor, but every time I try it, it sounds completely wrong. If I'm right, the melodic minor is merely a major scale with a flattened third and so how can it be so important if the only 'dissonant' note is the flat third? I want to get into playing a bit of jazz, but I feel I'm knocking on the wrong door completely here.

**A:** As far as jazz improvisation is concerned, there are two ways of learning it: you either pick it up instinctively or you have to apply some sort of method. One way or another the ear has to sort jazz's rich variety of scale, chord and chromatic tones into some sort of order and become adept at using them in a melodic context. If you're lucky, you'll pick this up by ear – if not, you have to condition the ear, introducing it to the vocabulary of improvisation by exploring different musical areas – and one is the melodic minor scale.

It's true to say that, in its basic form, this scale differs from the major by one degree – and if you try to apply it randomly it simply won't fit and will sound severely out of place. This is because the way that the sound of the melodic minor is heard is principally modal – that is to say that it isn't played from root to root.

Arguably it's the seventh mode of the melodic minor – also known as the Superlocrian – which gets the heaviest wear in jazz as it contains all of the notes which are commonly referred to as the 'outside tones' (see diagrams). If we analyse this mode of the scale, you can see that it contains the root, ♭9, ♯9, 3rd, ♭5th ♯5th and ♭7, which offers up a heady cocktail of altered tones. It is most commonly heard over a

dominant 7th chord, but its application implies a bit of what I call 'music maths' in that you have to effectively think in an entirely different key to the one you're playing.

For example, if you wanted to apply the Superlocrian over a C7 chord, you'd have to play the melodic minor starting on C♯ in order to get the right mode. I've always fought against this kind of thinking as I believe it can confuse people unnecessarily (believe me, I've seen it happen!) and players who have been taught this way can end up merely playing the scale in an almost Pavlovian fashion, rather than creating a melody from it, if you see the distinction.

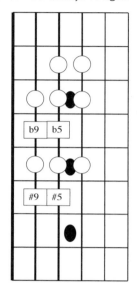

**Mixolydian scale with the position of altered tones marked**

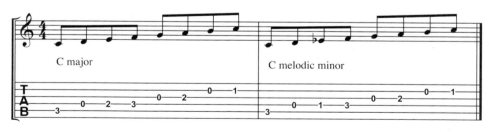

C major

C melodic minor

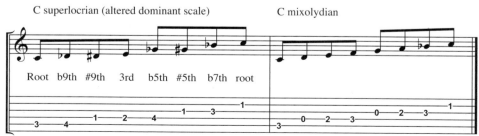

C superlocrian (altered dominant scale)

C mixolydian

Root  b9th  #9th   3rd   b5th  #5th  b7th  root

My own take on the situation is that you can create an altered scale sound by learning where the chromatic tones lie within the Mixolydian mode; if you already know the fingering for a C Mixolydian then it's only a small step to understand where the chromatic tones lie within it and this inspires creativity rather than something which is, to me, almost wholly artificial.

**Q:** I'm in the middle of reading a book on guitar music theory and it says that you can play an E minor pentatonic scale over a C major chord. Why? Surely you'd play the C major pentatonic or perhaps the minor if it was a bit bluesy.

**A:** It's all a question of interpretation. When you're first introduced to pentatonic shapes you learn that there are five for each minor key and five for each major.

Once you've sorted out where the different roots are you commit each to memory and think the job's finished. Then someone comes along and messes with your mind by telling you that there are more pentatonic shapes to consider!

What we have here is one of those situations where, technically speaking, the E minor pentatonic will fit over C major, but only because the notes it contains happen to be in the key of C (see example below). But the resulting notes – E G A B and D – are nothing to do with the actual C major pentatonic scale itself, which is made up from the notes C D E G and A. So it's true to say that E minor pentatonic 'fits over C major' but only from the point of view that the notes therein are 'key friendly' – you won't get that familiar major pentatonic sound if you try superimposing E minor over C. However, you're welcome to experiment – you might come up with some very good sounding licks that way.

**Q:** I'm trying to understand keys and the scales you can play over the top of various chords, but I keep coming across songs where most of the chords fit the key but there are one or two that definitely don't. How come they don't sound strange or out of place and what do I have to do to play over the top?

**A:** Basically, there are seven chords in each major key which are built up from the individual notes in the parent scale. If a melody stays within the confines of a single key (and plenty of them do) then we can harmonise or accompany that melody using a selection of appropriate chords from amongst these seven.

It's usually either the chords built on the first, fourth and fifth degrees or, in jazz circles, chords built on the first, second and fifth as these chords will support an entire melody based on a single scale.

This has resulted in some memorable melodies in the past, but composers are an adventurous lot and always trying to put the occasional melodic 'S bend' in their compositions which means looking outside the scale and introducing the occasional 'visitor' to the proceedings.

This means using a chord that doesn't fit in with the key, often used in support of a tone from outside the parent scale.

Usually, these visiting tonalities only sustain for a short while – otherwise we'd actually perceive them as a key change – meaning that there's often a slight bump in the road when you come to improvise over the top. For jazz musicians this is a way of life as many jazz standards include 'visitor chords' but it can take a while to get used to at first.

To begin with you need to know exactly what extra notes the visiting chord or chords are bringing to the parent scale. For instance, if you find an A7 cropping up in a song in the key of C, a quick analysis shows that the only note present in the chord which isn't in the C scale is C# and so you would have to acknowledge this when playing over the top. It might sound like a hard slog at first, but you end up being able to do this almost entirely by ear.

A7 in C major? The C# is 'just visiting'!

**Q:** Can you offer any tips on how to learn to play 'late', i.e. just behind the beat?

**A:** This is all to do with learning to play with feel in general. What I advise students to do when asked a question like this myself is to play me an example of what they mean from a CD.

Once we find a good specimen, I either transcribe it or find them a transcription and go through it with them inch by inch. Once the student has got the basic notes down, I encourage them to play along with the CD until their version matches the recorded one exactly. It also helps if they sing the part, too as many melody lines or solos tend to follow our very human sense of phrasing which stems from breath patterns. This way, they can 'feel' what's going on, rather than trying to determine it from the printed page.

I'd recommend that you come up with a few examples of 'late' playing from your own CD collection and then begin to track down some transcriptions and follow the procedure outlined above.

You'll soon begin to understand what's happening this way.

**Q:** Can you explain what an 'inversion' is with regard to chords? Surely most guitar chords must be some kind of inversion as they are very rarely root, third and fifth as they would be on a piano.

**A:** Very simply, a chord's basic structure in 'root position' is considered to be as you describe it yourself – root, third and fifth. If these three notes are presented in any other order, the chord is said to be an 'inversion'.

If, for instance, the chord is spelled 3rd, 5th, root, it is said to be in 'first inversion'. If the

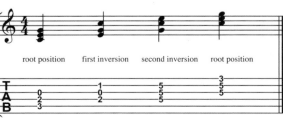

root position    first inversion    second inversion    root position

5th is in the bass – 5th, root 3rd – then it's known as a 'second inversion'.

As you suspect, many guitar chords have the notes jumbled up in them and so they don't really conform to text book ideas, but it's a good idea from the point of view of ear training at least, to work out and listen to some triads with the third or fifth in the bass just to get some idea of the effect they have musically.

**Q:** What's a 'blue third', exactly? I often see it referred to in tutors, but I'm not sure where to find it on the guitar neck.

**A:** A blue third is a term used to describe the sound of the third in the blues scale. For various historical reasons this particular note doesn't correspond to western ideas of pitch as it sits on the fence in between our conception of major and minor thirds – literally. The blue third is the sharp side of a minor third and the flat side of a major third.

What this means to us as guitar players is that we usually fret the minor third in the blues scale and bend it very slightly – approximately a quarter tone – to achieve the desired effect.

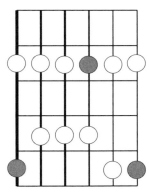

The shaded notes on the fretboard diagram above will all benefit from being bent slightly sharp.

**Q:** I keep seeing players looking at their left-hand fingers while they perform – is this something you believe should be avoided and, if so, how do you train yourself to get out of the habit?

**A:** Let's put it this way – it doesn't look too good, does it? Imagine yourself out in the audience – what would you rather see, a guitarist looking down at his hand all evening or someone communicating with the audience?

To be honest, it's a difficult habit to break, as we all learn it early on in our playing lives when positioning the fingers is awkward and ungainly. And we're quite likely to continue the habit unless something else comes along to distract us in the meantime. So what to do?

One thing is to make a conscious effort to look between your hands so that you have both in sight at once – this will at least make it look like you're looking ahead into the mid-distance from an audience perspective. It will come with training, but may take time.

Another way is to give yourself something else to look at – which will involve forcing yourself to play more by 'feel' than by sight. I've suggested that students try looking at themselves in a reflective surface in order to learn to look away (it sounds vain, but it does work as they can still see their left hands, but don't have to look down to do so).

Alternatively, learn some songs from a songbook placed on a stand positioned slightly to your left so that you can see your left-hand fingers using your peripheral vision. This will begin the process of 'looking away' for you, too.

I believe that it's quite important to learn not to rely on visual information as quite often what you see can hold you back (for instance, there is not much difference in terms of 'feel' between playing in C major or D flat major – but if your eyes catch sight of you playing in the 'unfamiliar' area of D flat on the fretboard, it can send panic signals to the brain!). If you learn instead to listen to what you're doing you'll find that certain areas of your playing can improve.

**Q:** I hear the most wonderful guitar parts in my head all the time, but I can't yet play them when I pick up a guitar. Is there a way to make this link actually work?

**A:** You need to indulge in some serious ear training. At the moment, what you're hearing in your head is akin to listening to a foreign radio broadcast – you can't make out the language – and so you need to learn the language of music from an aural – as opposed to technical – point of view.

There are downloadable ear training programmes available on the internet and this would be a very good place to begin. The other thing is to learn to transcribe – it sounds frightening, I know, but don't set yourself impossible tasks. Begin with some really easy nursery rhymes and find the melodies on your guitar by ear – one note at a time. Hum each note and keep humming it until you find it with your fingers. Then move on to the next note, and so on. It sounds painfully slow, but you'll find that by gradually making inroads into the aural language of music in this way, the music in your head will stop sounding foreign and unobtainable, and start becoming within reach.

**Q:** I just don't seem to be getting anywhere with my playing – there are still loads of things I can't do. What can I do to motivate myself?

**A:** It seems to be a human trait that, instead of celebrating what we've achieved so far, we look forward to the road ahead and bemoan the work we have to do in the future!

Basically, you need to make some changes to your practice routine, which has probably been allowed to become stale and directionless. Sit down and write yourself out a daily regime that you will stick to – begin with some warm ups, move on to some scale exercises, then set some time apart for learning new material, whether it's in the form of playing over backing tracks or studying transcriptions. You should find that the fresh input goes a long way towards revitalising your playing.

# 4: MEDICAL MATTERS

*I've been asked loads of questions about the physical and biological aspects of playing. When you think about it, we all rely on biology in order to develop as players – muscle has to grow, tendons have to play their part, joints have to flex – and so it's not really something that any of us can afford to ignore for long. Often when I'm asked by a student, 'Why can't I do this?' the answer is that nature hasn't yet provided sufficient muscle power or flexibility and that only time and patient practice will save the day.*

*Another aspect that is increasingly common among guitarists now is repetitive strain injury and other associated aliments. Today's guitar playing can be very demanding on the body and so it's wise to arm yourself with ways to avoid unnecessary trips to the doctor...*

**Q:** My hands are large and I find that I don't fret chords and arpeggios cleanly on my six string. Are all guitar fretboards designed with the same width between strings? Can you suggest a similar guitar which does have greater width between the strings?

**A:** You'd be surprised how little hand size affects guitar playing in general. I've personally taught students with a vast variety of physical hand sizes and they've all been able to adapt to a standard size of guitar neck.

I would recommend that you persevere, but if all else fails, classical guitar necks, some older acoustics and jazz semi acoustics tend to have wider fretboards. Some of the old blues players used to use 12-string guitars strung with six strings to give them the extra width, too.

**Q:** Fingerpicking shreds my fingernails. Is there anything I can put on to protect them without appearing like a complete girl?

**A:** Poor strength and durability in fingernails can be a symptom of poor diet as they are made up from keratin, the same protein found in skin and hair. It can also be down to something as simple as bad manicure habits, too. I suggest you spend a few minutes on the internet researching nail care and the implications of diet before you trot off in search of any magic remedies. But, if you're sure that your general health is in good shape, then there are plenty of preparations available that will strengthen nails – albeit artificially. A trip to your local Boots (take your sister / wife / girlfriend / mother along for camouflage if you're shy) will reveal most of them. Failing that, and if you're feeling particularly brave, nail bars are opening on high streets all over our fair land and they will be only too willing to offer advice on what's available in the specialist field to help get those talons back up to strength.

**Q:** If someone has minor tendonitis in their fretting hand, would really light strings (for bending and vibrato) and smaller frets and neck size (for ease with stretching) really help them? Is there a particular guitar, string set and instrument maker that you could recommend for something like this?

**A:** To begin with, I'd ask you to read the section below, written by my friend Dr James Cameron. However, my advice where 'mild' tendonitis is concerned is to treat the problem itself and not just try to live around the symptoms. Tendonitis can be treated – it's usually a question of rest, perhaps a bit of heat treatment and taking the advice from a doctor who is fully sympathetic with the cause. With time, the condition should clear up and everything will be fine.

The most important thing is to consider what caused the problem in the first place. Usually, this kind of situation is caused by bad posture when practising; we all do it – frantically playing scales whilst slumped in front of the TV with the wrist in an awkward position. If you're prone to painful wrists whilst playing ask yourself why and – literally – take a good look in the mirror. Are your wrists as straight as possible? Are you wearing your guitar strap (fashionably) too low forcing you to adopt a poor posture? Are your forearms relaxed? Are your shoulders hunched? Do you feel yourself tense up when trying to play a fast run? Asking questions like this should start providing clues to what caused the condition and rethinking your playing posture will prevent a recurrence.

**Q:** **I haven't been playing for very long and I have what I think is a very unusual problem. I have quite short, stubby fingers on both hands and find it very difficult to fret chords cleanly. I always seem to be muting out strings because my fingers are getting in the way of each other on the fretboard. Is this something that I can get around or should I just give up now?**

**A:** Not so unusual, worry not! In my years as a teacher I have seen fingers of all shapes and sizes and have never found anything that prevented a particular pupil from learning to play successfully, despite their fears to the contrary. In the early stages of playing, it's always more a question of gaining dexterity in the left hand. The thing is that the left-hand fingers have probably done nothing more dextrous than hold a cup or operate a gear stick, and need some training before they can perform the choreography necessary to change from one chord shape to another.

Just keep practising and every time you hear a muted or unclear note, stop and make

some minor adjustments to your finger position and things should slowly improve.

**Q:** **I have been experiencing considerable pain in the back of my left hand and my wrist (especially when stretching for chords). I have been playing for three years and I don't think I'm doing anything different from before, my thumb is straight and my hands relaxed yet I still get this pain. I don't want it to keep me from guitar but at the moment it hurts to even pick it up.**

**A:** I think the advice has to be to see a doctor immediately. Stop playing until you've sought medical advice as serious pain like this is an indication that something is very wrong – you've probably heard of medical conditions like repetitive strain injury and tendonitis, for example (see opposite) – and we could be looking at something like this. These two conditions can be treated if they're caught soon enough, but the only real remedy is to take a rest from playing for a while. The important thing here is to see a doctor immediately and don't take any risks along the way.

**Q:** **Recently I have started doing some fingering exercises which have improved my left-hand dexterity. Unfortunately during those exercises my left hand and wrist feel very uncomfortable, even painful sometimes. What would be a correct placement of the left hand? Should the thumb be in the middle of the neck, pointing upwards or should it be hooked over the top? Should the wrist be straight or should it be angled? Should the elbow touch the rest of the body? Should the guitar be placed in the middle of the body or slightly to the side? (I practise standing up.) What should be happening to the thumb as one moves up/down the neck (doing a chromatic run for example).**

**A:** The correct position for the left hand is to keep the wrist as straight as possible in order to avoid potential problems with tendonitis and other associated ailments. Thumb position varies, depending on how high or low you wear your strap – it's only in the classical world that it stays pretty much fixed in the middle of the neck. The important thing is that it should act as a support to the fingers on the fretboard and so try to keep it as vertical as you can at all times. The thumb acts as a guide for the fingers as they move over the fretboard, but should not 'grip' the neck or drag behind the fingers.

As far as the elbow is concerned, it should not tuck itself into the body as this implies some sort of tension present somewhere in the arm whereas it should remain as relaxed as possible.

Actual guitar position varies from player to player, but a consensus should be easy to come by after looking at a few pictures of players in guitar publications and comparing their stances to your own while looking in a mirror.

**Q:** **I have been playing guitar for about four and a half years now; I really got into the guitar two years ago when I started a music course at college. Since then I have been playing guitar intensively, and buying every good guitar magazine available so I can be the best guitarist I possibly can. However over the last month I have developed a bad repetitive strain injury in my right arm and a lesser pain in my left arm too. I wondered if a repetitive strain injury now (aged 18) will crush my aspirations to become a successful professional guitarist in the future. Any advice would be very much appreciated.**

**A:** My advice regarding RSI is always the same; you need to seek medical advice immediately and be prepared to give playing a rest for a while to give the body a chance to heal. It's only by following this course that you will give yourself the possibility of playing professionally in the future.

Meanwhile, check out your playing stance as

repetitive strain injury is nearly always down to bad posture or invalid practice habits – remember, you must warm up before tackling anything technically challenging to give the muscles a chance to condition themselves first. As I have said before, if you wear your strap fashionably low it can cause back problems as well as wrist and forearm pain owing to the fact that the wrists are far too angled – they should be as straight as possible. Fashion isn't worth risking your health for, in my opinion!

**Q:** **You're probably going to think this is a silly question, but I've been playing for a few months and the fingers on my left hand are really sore where they hold down the strings. I know that they'll harden up eventually, but how long does this take? And is there any way I can speed things up in this respect? Sometimes when I pick my guitar up my fingers are too sore to play and it's very frustrating. Please help!**

**A:** The amount of time it takes to harden up the fingertips varies enormously and there are a lot of factors that will contribute one way or another.

When I was learning, rumours abounded as to what players did to harden up their fingertips. Everything from rubbing them on brick to soaking them in vinegar and beyond, I seem to remember.

But in the end I have to say that I haven't found anything better than good old practice to get those calluses forming – even if you have to follow the 'everything in moderation' rule and resist being tempted to overdo things or rush nature. We've all been there, suffered the blisters and peeling skin, but the skin has thickened up like elephant hide in due course!

The only thing I will mention is that it might be a good idea to get your guitar checked over to make sure things like string gauge and playing action aren't acting as a barrier to progress.

**Q:** I started playing a long time ago and gave it up when my life got too busy to keep up with the practising. Now I've got a bit of space again I've recently picked it up, but I've found that the handful of chords I learned back then, which I still remember, were all learned with a bad thumb position and now I can't get anywhere. Does this mean I have to go back to the beginning and re-learn everything with the correct thumb position?

**A:** It all depends on how we define 'bad thumb position'. A common error amongst beginners is to lay the thumb flat along the back of the neck so that it's pointing towards the headstock, instead of having it vertical. This means that the fingers on the fretboard are not properly supported and positioning chords correctly with the fingers is rendered very difficult. If this is the case here, then I would say that you definitely have to go back to basics and adjust your thumb position before proceeding any further.

As a general rule, the thumb should only move between 'five to' or 'five past' the vertical – anything more and it isn't really doing the job properly.

*So much for questions I'm actually qualified to answer. For the rest, however, I asked Dr. James Cameron to give some pointers about musculoskeletal injuries in guitarists and what we can do to avoid them. Dr. Cameron has experience of diagnosing and treating these conditions and, as a guitarist himself, offers advice on how to avoid problems developing. Remember, this advice is general and may not be appropriate for everyone. Always discuss any problems or symptoms with your own doctor.*

*Whether you're a professional or hobby guitarist, you will recognise the need for regular practice in order to improve. However, guitarists – as well as other musicians – are one of several special risk groups for repetitive motion injuries. The association between using computer keyboards and repetitive strain injury is perhaps the most commonly known, but painful wrist conditions in musicians are receiving more attention in the medical community. One survey of 250 musicians revealed that approximately half currently had some musculoskeletal symptoms, and almost all had experienced symptoms at some time.*

**Q:** Can guitarists really get injured?

**A:** 'Making music is an act which is as physical as it is mental. A special type of fitness and stamina is required and it is no wonder that under such a strain the body can be hurt in one way or another. The hands and arms of a musician are his most precious possessions; but are highly vulnerable to abuse and injury.

Instrumental injuries include the same conditions experienced from computer overuse – carpal tunnel syndrome, tendonitis, tenosynovitis and others. But the particular demands of playing guitar can produce other problems as well. Incorrect posture, non-ergonomic technique, excessive force, overuse and insufficient rest all contribute to chronic injuries that can cause great pain, disability and the end of some careers.'

**Q:** Are we talking about repetitive strain injury?

**A:** 'Repetitive strain injury (RSI) is more of a description than a diagnosis. It is a muscular condition that arises as a result of excessive repetitive activity. It usually presents as pain or stiffness in the fingers, hands, wrists or forearms. Weakness, numbness, tingling or loss of strength and co-ordination may also be present.

The primary cause of RSI is overuse. However, many factors are involved in the progression of the condition. Factors such as physical fitness, individual work habits, stress, long hours, lack of breaks, bad ergonomics and poor, static posture can all play a part. Indeed, some people are physically stronger and can play for longer even with a tense technique, without incurring injury.

The mechanism behind developing RSI is thought to be a circulation problem. More tension in the muscles during repetitive use restricts the circulation to the muscles, tendons and nerves. Less blood flow means less oxygen gets to these tissues, making them susceptible to damage.

Tendonitis and tenosynovitis are terms meaning inflammation of the tendons and tendon sheaths respectively. They usually affect the tendons that flex the fingers, causing the condition known as 'trigger finger'. The characteristic symptom of this is to wake with one finger flexed and stiff, with occasionally a small nodule that can be felt just below the skin in the tendon itself.'

## Q: Is RSI treatable?

**A:** 'Treatment depends upon the cause, and how much damage has been done. In general, this involves reducing or stopping the activity which caused the problem, plus programmed exercise and physiotherapy. For the guitarist, this means no playing – a daunting prospect. The condition usually resolves with time, but in severe cases this can take years. Prevention is therefore a priority.

In tendonitis or tenosynovitis, treatment is likely to include anti-inflammatory medication. In addition a small injection of a corticosteroid preparation into a tendon nodule usually provides relief.'

## Q: What is Carpal Tunnel Syndrome?

**A:** 'Carpal tunnel syndrome is a more common condition, found in situations other than musicians' injuries; the most common being in pregnancy. It is caused

simply by too much pressure inside the wrist, compressing the important nerve that runs through the centre of the wrist joint – the median nerve. It causes pain or tingling in the hand, usually at night, followed by weakness of the small muscles at the base of the thumb.

Treatment involves wearing a splint at night or a steroid injection in the wrist for temporary relief. The syndrome usually resolves on its own, but in severe and unremitting cases, a small surgical procedure may be required to decompress the wrist, providing a complete cure. This is rarely required however; most cases being self-limiting.'

## Q: How do I tell the difference between normal aches and pains, and something that's doing me harm?

**A:** 'Pain is not normal. If what you are feeling is pain, then you are doing something wrong. Pain is your body's way of alerting you to damage being done to your body. The pain receptors in your joints and muscles are stimulated when there is inflammation or direct forceful injury. Even a mild 'ache' usually signifies some degree of strain on a muscle – an ankle sprain for example. If your hands or fingers or wrists are hurting whilst playing guitar, you MUST stop playing, and analyse what you are doing wrong. Severe injuries to the hands of musicians occur more often than you would imagine.

Other symptoms of these conditions include stiffness, numbness, tingling and loss of control. The most common symptom is wrist pain. In the event of one or more of the symptoms described above developing, then seek medical advice early. Don't be reluctant to go in case of finding out you have a serious injury; the chances are that you have a small sprain or something similar, and just need to reduce your playing for a while. If your doctor seems not to know much about RSI, then find one who does. To ensure a good outcome, these injuries have to be dealt with properly.'

**Q:** Does being diagnosed with tendonitis mean I've got to stop playing?

**A:** 'Reducing your playing is important when any symptoms develop. Complete rest of your hands is probably not the best solution, so do some simple hand work, but yes, abstaining from playing guitar is a must.

Anti-inflammatory medication may be useful, but only when suggested by your doctor. In severe cases, your doctor may suggest some other forms of therapy, such as physiotherapy, which is an excellent first-line treatment. A good programme will include neck and shoulder massage, as well as forearm massage. A type of physiotherapy called adverse mechanical tension physiotherapy is rapidly effective and has been recommended by people who have previously had RSI.

A good programme of physiotherapy, along with a reduction in playing, is usually enough to abolish your symptoms; however, to prevent recurrence, it is vital to evaluate your playing and perhaps work on some relaxation techniques.'

**Q:** I'm getting an ache in my wrists after playing for twenty minutes or so. What could I be doing wrong?

**A:** 'You need to evaluate your technique. This is very important. The aim is not to re-train yourself to play the guitar in some 'proper' fashion, but to find areas in your playing that require attention. Reducing the tension in your fingers while you play is a good place to start. Try and relax as you play – this may actually improve your playing as well as help prevent injury. Take lots of breaks to stretch and relax; both momentary breaks every few minutes and longer breaks every hour or so. This seems a particularly obvious piece of advice, and yet so many guitarists will play and play without taking any breaks, and then wonder why their hands are aching.

Keep your arms and hands warm. Cold muscles are at much greater risk for overuse injuries. Warm-up exercises are ideal – simple patterns on the guitar are a good way to get your fingers gently warmed up and ready for playing. No athlete would get out of bed and start running immediately without warming-up his muscles. You should treat your hand and finger muscles with the same respect.

Evaluate your posture when playing. Whether standing or sitting, your posture can influence your health as well as your playing. Some guidelines would include: keeping your shoulders relaxed and allowing your elbows to swing free. Keep your wrists as straight as possible. Some traditional classical guitar styles are quite tough on your wrists, encouraging bent, rather than straight wrists. Try not to slouch or slump forward; and pull your chin in to look down – don't flop your head forward. Keep the hollow in the base of your spine and, very importantly, alter your position from time to time. Try and make a conscious effort not to allow any part of your body to remain totally rigid for any length of time.'

**Q:** My doctor suggested meditation. How can that help?

**A:** 'Relaxation techniques, from simple breathing exercises to patented techniques (Alexander, Feldenkrais), are proven to be especially beneficial in these injuries. Relaxation and stress management have shown themselves to decrease the incidence of RSI-type injuries as well as aiding in their treatment.

A type of posture relaxation technique is the Alexander technique. It is a therapy designed to give you more control over your activities, by increasing your awareness of your body. Focusing on areas such as relaxing your neck muscles, it is an active and comprehensive relaxation programme, and has been shown to have positive psychological effects as well as health benefits.

By working hard at these relaxation techniques, it makes it less likely that you will resume your old bad habits. The time and commitment required by all these treatments appears a little excessive, until you remember how essential it is to have functioning hands. This is serious stuff; it's one of those things that no-one ever thinks will happen to them, until one day they end up unable to play their instrument; and to dedicated musicians that is a tragedy.'

**Q:** Is it true that wearing gloves after playing a gig helps protect the muscles?

**A:** 'Cold muscles are vulnerable, which is why warm-ups are important. Equally, sudden cooling of your hands after playing a gig could be hazardous, but unless you plan to put your hands in cold water, or your gig is in an Arctic country, gloves probably aren't necessary.'

**Q:** Can alcohol or caffeine have any effect on your muscles?

**A:** 'Dehydration is particularly bad for your muscles. Your body tissues are composed mostly of water, and dehydration can impair your ability and control, as well as inhibit the healing process. Caffeinated and alcoholic drinks both dehydrate you, so should generally be avoided. The stimulating affect of caffeine will also tense your muscles. Better is to drink plenty of water – at least one glass per hour.'

**Q:** Which muscles have to develop in order to gain the strength/agility to play well?

**A:** 'Upper body strength is important. But this doesn't mean going to a gym three times a week to 'pump iron' – much better is to improve your posture and perhaps having a good general exercise programme of stretching and gentle movements. I often recommend Tai Chi to friends and patients.

Obviously, the fine control of your fingers is crucial to a musician, and this requires a different approach. The pattern of muscle contractions and relaxations to move a finger in a precise way is quite complex. It's helpful to understand the basic anatomy of the musculature in your arm and hand.

Two quick definitions first – a tendon is the tough fibrous structure that connects muscle to bone. A ligament is a similar structure, but connects bone to other bones only. Ligament injuries are called sprains. Tendon (or muscle) injuries are called strains.

There are numerous muscles involved in moving your fingers about. The first subdivision is into the extrinisic and intrinsic muscles.

Extrinsic muscles: These are the long muscles in your forearm, with long tendons which pass through your wrist and up to insert into the bones of your fingers. The group on the 'palm' side of your forearm are the 'flexors', and on the outside of your forearm, the 'extensors'.

You've probably guessed this already, but the flexors flex your fingers, and the extensors extend them! Test this yourself... lay your arm on the table, and flex your fingers whilst watching your forearm. You will see the muscles contract and move about. These groups of muscles work hard during all wrist and hand activities. They are the muscles most frequently injured – whether the muscles themselves or the tendon attachments.

Intrinsic muscles: These are the much smaller muscles, lying completely within your hand. They are the lumbricals and the interosseus muscles. There are several of them, and they control the side-to-side and fine movements of the fingers. This makes them very important muscles for the guitarist. They are less frequently damaged, but do need the same care and attention.

'Finger memory' is a familiar concept to the musician – the almost subconscious thought process that allows your fingers to take up certain position to play notes or chords in a previously learned way. This process relies on your intrinsic muscles being well trained and well looked after.'

**Q: Is there anything I can do to speed up the process of development?**

**A:** 'The best way to progress, as recommended by most guitar teachers, is to develop an efficient and useful practice regime. We are all guilty of the 30-minute 'practice' that actually consists of playing the two or three tunes we always play, playing a few random chords, and that's it. How will that sort of program ever develop our playing technique and dexterity?

Much better is to establish a set program of warm-ups and stretching exercises, perhaps by playing scales or other patterns on the fretboard. Then some musical pieces that increase in complexity and demands on your fingers.

This is not an overnight process, and for some people it may take many weeks or even months to see progress. Be cautious not to become a victim of overuse. Again, if you are getting any pains or other symptoms in your hands and forearms during practice, then stop and work out what you are doing wrong. Is your position or technique in need of adjustment, or are you just overdoing it, and need to reduce your practice time and take more breaks?'

**Q: Why are my little fingers so hard to control? They seem to want to follow my third fingers around...**

**A:** 'Our little fingers tend to be neglected, not just in guitar playing but in a lot of manual activities. They tend not to develop the strength of the other fingers, nor the minute control and dexterity. In some people, even their independence seems to have vanished and they barely function as a separate finger!

Anyone who has studied classical guitar will recognise the letters p, i, m and a for right-hand fingering instructions. I can't even remember if there's a letter for the little finger! *(In fact, there is – a small letter 'c' – DM)* Traditional technique places the thumb for the bass, and the next three fingers on the three treble strings, leaving the little finger floating in the air. Some guitarists have developed a technique (not recommended) of anchoring their right-hand little finger on the guitar body, just below the sound-hole (or pickups).

There is a common misbelief that the reason for the little finger's lack of control is that it shares a tendon with the ring finger, unlike the thumb, index and middle which all have their own tendons, thus rendering it a close buddy of the ring finger, and unable to move about much on its own. This is nonsense and reflects a very poor and over-simplistic understanding of wrist and forearm muscular anatomy.

The little finger has the same attachments to the flexor and extensor muscles as the other fingers, and has the same intrinsic muscles helping its control and precise movements. In fact, your little finger and index finger have one additional muscle and tendon each, that the other two fingers lack – the extensor digiti minimi and extensor indicis muscles. If you're interested in learning more about this fascinating subject of hand anatomy, there are websites galore to discover, and of course medical bookshops/libraries full of anatomy texts – usually with pictures!

So, no more excuses for your little finger. It has the potential to be another useful digit in your playing. To develop little finger strength and dexterity on the guitar, simply invent exercises that use it. For example, for your left-hand little finger, play simple chromatic scales along each string... first finger first fret, then second finger second fret, third finger third fret and fourth/little finger fourth fret. Play across all strings. Play in a different sequence. Move about across the strings. Increase the speed – and practise it every day.

I don't really recommend these spring-loaded hand-grip exercise things – I don't think they really improve the co-ordinated strength you require for guitar playing, and I've not yet heard anyone claim differently.'

**Q:** I'm left handed – should I try to play right handed first?

**A:** 'There are many different opinions on this. There are several advantages to playing 'right-handed', not least the availability of instruments! From a medical point of view, I'm not sure there is any specific advice. Whatever feels comfortable and 'right' would seem to be the way. Get advice from an experienced guitar teacher who has taught left-handed people.'

**Q:** My fingernails break all the time – what can I do?

**A:** 'Not many of us are blessed with talons for fingernails, unfortunately. Many of the performing acoustic guitarists I know use some kind of nail treatment or polish to harden the nail and prevent it breaking, with Superglue handy for emergency repairs! Stick-on nails or painted on acrylic reinforcement are also popular, though I do wonder if the glue actually has a negative effect on the nail underneath.

A piece of advice I once received was to never cut your nails, just use a nail file, and file them daily. Some people recommend vitamin supplements of various kinds, though I doubt there is any evidence for this.'

# 5: A JOB IN MUSIC?

*We all know that the music industry is a place where, notoriously, the big fish eat the little fish – and when we start out we're all plankton. Literally, we're at the bottom of the food chain and the only way is up. But it's a big old ocean and the sooner you get out there and start swimming the better. The recurring theme around the subject of gaining employment in the music business is that of communication – the old adage 'it's not what you know' is absolutely true. I resisted the idea for years, but every success I've had – and I mean every success – has been because I knew the right person to call – and the vital thing was that they knew me, too.*

*So in this chapter we will be dealing with the question of gaining some sort of employment that involves having a guitar in your hands, whether it be teaching, playing for shows or session work...*

*I'm going to ignore the job of 'rock star' because, to be honest, nothing I could tell you would necessarily prepare you for that role. All the people I've interviewed for magazines over the years have all had a different tale to tell, regarding how they made their debut in professional music – many have been published in my book* Talking Guitars, *if you're interested to see just how many different doors there are into the business.*

*I think it was the late DJ John Peel who likened advising people how to embark on a career in music to telling someone how to get struck by lightening. 'All you can really do,' he said, 'is to tell them to hang around in wide open spaces during a thunderstorm...' And, as you can probably guess, even after taking that kind of advice, it's still an almost completely random affair!*

*So let's take a closer look at various avenues of professional music-making, beginning with teaching. I was a private tutor for most of the 1980s, as well as teaching in a few local schools. On the whole, I enjoyed the experience enormously, although in retrospect, it meant that I was side-tracked into ignoring my own career as a player. It's a strange thing, but once you become known as a teacher, many people forget that you can actually play!*

**Q:** **Can anyone set up teaching privately from home or do they have to have some sort of qualification?**

**A:** You don't need a qualification as such, no, but I would say that the competition out there is probably quite high and so the more you can do to distinguish yourself from the rest of the teaching crowd, the better.

When I began teaching back in the 1980s, there weren't the colleges around that there are now and so gaining a diploma or degree in actually teaching 'modern' steel string guitar was pretty much impossible anyway.

I merely placed an advert in the local paper, went round the local music shops leaving my details and sat back to wait for the phone to ring – which, luckily, it did.

Obviously in order to build up a teaching roster big enough to enable you to live off your earnings you have to make yourself known and it took me a while to get my level of advertising just right. I began by choosing to advertise in the once-a-week local paper, but soon found that this was expensive and not particularly cost effective. So, in the end, I went for an ad in the local 'free' paper, because that way the ad was still visible once every seven days but it didn't cost too much to have it in there week after week. My advice here would be to ignore everything the telephone sales staff who deal with placing your ad will tell you – they work on commission and obviously want you to have the most expensive advert available. Don't.

Go for something that is simple, direct and in plain sight – I put mine in with the 'Musical Instruments' because I (correctly) assumed that people who were enthusiastically looking for guitars would look there first – and they might not even bother looking at the 'Tutors' section (which was full of 'learn French' or 'Maths taught at home' type of ads). I was depending on someone going looking for some bargain equipment and my ad placing the notion in their minds that it might be good to go for a couple of lessons.

As I say, it must have worked, because I ended up teaching six days a week and had a sizeable waiting list as well within only a short time.

But that was back in the 1980s and things have changed. The first major change is the internet and I would say that it is now almost essential for anyone hoping to go into private teaching seriously to get themselves a domain name and have a site designed to display your wares. It's up to you what you do with it, but having a look around should give you some ideas. I have a surf around every so often and there are definitely some teachers out there with some good ideas.

Some have free lessons available on their sites so you can 'try before you buy'. The thing to do is look around and take note, then draw from the best.

One thing which is just beginning to happen now, thanks to broadband connections becoming commonplace, is actual lessons over the internet. If you have a camera connected to your computer, you can pay for a lesson from someone living 4,000 miles away in the US – without even having to leave your house. Technology, when it works, never ceases to amaze me.

**Q:** What advice would you give someone who wanted to teach from home?

**A:** Keep an open mind and don't slip down the easy route of having an inflexible teaching programme. Be honest, too; no one expects you to know everything and so if someone comes to you asking about an area of playing that you're really not up to speed with, tell them. Don't say that they really shouldn't consider that area as it's uncommercial, or 'too difficult' or some such twaddle, just because you only want to teach them your own favourite style, because you won't earn their respect – or keep their custom for very long – by doing so.

I always told my pupils that if I didn't know the answer to something, I would tell them. The chances were that I knew where I could find the answer, as long as they would bear with me, but I didn't try to distract them away from their own course of learning by deceiving them.

I worked to the principle that music is music – and a pupil will get on much quicker and more enthusiastically if you teach them the material they want to know. For instance, if someone came in wanting to learn material by The Smiths, then that was the way we went. All I asked was that they did some technical exercises like scales and so on first so that I could ensure that their technical development was on track.

In this way, I split the lesson so that we'd play through scales against the metronome for the first ten minutes of the lesson and then I would say, 'Right, what do you want to learn this week?' Usually, I would then be presented with either a songbook or a CD with the request, 'I'd like to learn the solo from such-and-such...' and I'd work it out for them, show them how to play it and write it down so they could take it home and practise it. In this way, I enjoyed the lesson because I was kept very much on my toes as a musician and was being exposed to a lot of music I might otherwise not have heard and my pupils went away happy because they were learning the music they liked.

More importantly, this way around, music lessons were fun and not some awful drudge where you end up being forced to learn music you can't stand merely because it's the way your teacher has been working for the last 30 years.

During the course of an average evening I would teach students who were into Hank Marvin, Stevie Ray Vaughan, Slayer and Eric Clapton. Quite a varied cross section of guitar styles!

**Q:** What sort of thing do you do on a first lesson with a pupil?

**A:** The first lesson is when you get to assess where you are going to start with a student. They might come to you completely fresh from the music store, having just bought their first guitar – a blank canvas – and so you start from the very beginning with simple chords and tips on keeping the guitar in tune, etc. Alternatively, you're quite likely to find that someone has been playing for a few months or even a couple of years, but they really haven't got beyond the basics and need some sort of guidance to the next level. This probably represents the bulk of the people I taught – they were 'stuck' and needed unsticking!

So I would ask them about the music they enjoyed listening to and ask them if they had learned any songs, and then perhaps ask them if I could wave a magic wand and have them leave the room playing like a particular player who would it be? Their answers usually were enough to give me a foothold into where I would start. We would then look at some simple scales or chords, but I would always angle it towards their tastes in music and try to show them that it was worth coming to terms with the technical side of playing because it would allow them to access the music they wanted to learn far quicker.

It's a good idea to get a clear picture of what a pupil's level of aspiration is, too. Do they want to play in public or just for their own amusement? Have they considered joining a band one day? I found that the main bulk of my students wanted to do one thing, all things considered; they wanted to learn any song of their choosing and be able to play it well reasonably quickly. This meant that they had to have a certain level of technique available to them and a system for assimilating new material, which were both tools I tried to pass on over a course of lessons, ever mindful that the journey I was taking them on should remain fun.

**Q:** How do I know how much to charge for a lesson?

**A:** To begin with, the Musicians' Union sets a sort of national minimum rate and so checking with them would be a good place to start. The other thing to do is to find out what other people charge for lessons in your area and aim to match them. The trick is not to appear 'cheap', whilst not vaulting towards the deluxe class either.

Obviously a 'known' local player can charge more for his services, and someone who is known at a national level can pretty much name their own price.

It's a fact that most people have no idea what sort of charges they are going to have to face from their guitar teacher. For some reason they expect you to be cheaper than the guy who has just fixed their plumbing or serviced their car, though! I once had to call out a plumber to fix a leaky washing machine. He was in the house for a total of 20 minutes and charged me £70 for the privilege – I never felt awkward about what I charged for lessons afterwards!

**Q:** I hear that there are now grade exams and even a diploma in electric guitar – how do I find out more details?

**A:** To begin with, there is an organisation in the UK called the Registry of Guitar Tutors which teachers can join – they also administer one of the available systems of grade exams. So I asked Tony Skinner, who runs the RGT, to answer a few questions concerning memberships and examinations:

**Q:** What are the benefits from registering with the RGT?

**A:** 'You can enhance your teaching status by offering students the opportunity of taking certificate examinations and gaining recognised qualifications as a result of their studies with you. Parents and schools are often particularly attracted by this possibility.

Your contact details and teaching styles can be listed in the *RGT Guitar Tutor Directory* which is widely distributed, as well as on the RGT website: www.RegistryOfGuitarTutors .com. This is an excellent way of increasing your roster of students and teaching work. (However, you can remain 'ex-directory', if you prefer.)

You will be sent an RGT Membership Certificate suitable for framing and display in your music teaching room.

You will receive three issues per year of *Guitar Tutor* magazine – the only publication aimed specifically at the needs and interests of all guitar teachers. This is full of useful information and advice about teaching methods and practices, reviews of teaching materials and much more.

You will have free access to the RGT's Tutor Advice and Support Service (TASS), enabling you to receive help and advice on all teaching matters from experienced educators.

You will be able to attend the RGT's Annual Guitar Teachers' Conference, as well as other courses and seminars for guitar teachers.

You can also obtain a wide range of music education books with substantial discounts on retail prices.'

**Q:** Is there some kind of screening for teachers who apply?

**A:** 'Yes, all applicants undergo a three-stage screening process. First, they have to complete an application form which details their teaching and playing experience, and requires them to declare any criminal convictions. It also asks them to list referees who can confirm their teaching experience.

Each applicant is then required to complete a skills specification form detailing the styles they teach and the level to which they teach them. Written references are then applied for and once all the documentation is received, it is reviewed by the RGT Director to assess the applicant's suitability for membership.

Those new to teaching may initially be offered 'associate' rather than full membership, meaning that their details will not be made publicly available by the RGT.'

**Q:** Do I need an actual qualification to belong to the RGT?

**A:** 'Applicants may apply on the basis of either professional playing and teaching experience or formal qualification.'

**Q:** What are the Grade Exams?

**A:** 'The RGT provides a comprehensive range of examinations that offer a formal recognition of the specific talents of electric guitar players. They range from Preliminary Grade (for beginners) up to Grade 8 (for aspiring professional musicians) plus a diploma level examination.

The electric guitar exams focus on practical music making and the skills you need to play in a band: chords, rhythm and lead solos.

Exams are also available for acoustic, bass and classical guitar.'

**Q:** Are the Grade Exams recognised by a music college?

**A:** 'The RGT exams are organised in partnership with London College of Music Exams (one of the world's most respected music examination boards, established in 1887) and certificated by

Thames Valley University, resulting in a recognised standard by which the skills and abilities of electric guitarists can be assessed.

All RGT graded exams are accredited by the Qualifications & Curriculum Authority (QCA) and have been placed on the National Qualifications Framework. UCAS points are awarded for RGT grades 6 to 8.

The examinations are also endorsed by a range of eminent guitarists from the fields of rock, jazz, pop and blues, including Sir Paul McCartney, Hank Marvin, David Gilmour and Ronnie Wood.'

**Q:** Is it possible to gain a diploma via the RGT?

**A:** 'Yes, in association with London College of Music Examinations, RGT offers a Licentiate Teacher's Diploma for electric guitar teachers. This legally entitles you to append the letters LLCM(TD) to your name.

For more information view the RGT website: www.RegistryOfGuitarTutors.com.'

**Q:** I want to attend one of the guitar colleges in my gap year from university – what sort of standard do I need to be in order to apply?

**A:** I asked Bruce Dickinson from the Brighton Institute of Modern Music (BIMM – www.bimm.co.uk) to fill in a few blanks in terms of attendance there...

**Q:** How good a player do I have to be to attend a guitar college?

**A:** 'To get the most out of it you need to be reasonably experienced – a full time course isn't for beginners. It's hard to generalise here, as guitarists are often very bad at judging their own abilities; but all the best colleges offer a one-to-one consultation so that's your chance to get some feedback on the strengths and weaknesses in your playing.'

**Q:** Is there an audition or entry exam I have to pass?

**A:** 'Yes, an audition where we will assess your technique, knowledge, general musicianship, experience and attitude. Nobody is perfect and we understand that many players are self taught and may be weak on say, theory, so it's not the end of the world if you fluff a few parts of the audition.'

**Q:** What sort of things will I learn?

**A:** 'There will be lectures such as technique, style, live performance, theory, sight reading, all taught by professional players with great CVs.

The main job is getting you to sound and carry yourself like a pro player. You may be surprised by the fact that playing simple stuff really well is actually just as hard as developing high-end technique.'

**Q:** Will I learn a lot of different styles of playing?

**A:** 'Yes; and you'll benefit from all of them, from jazz and fusion styles through to important creative players who often get overlooked in music colleges, such as Graham Coxon.'

**Q:** Do I come out with a qualification?

**A:** 'Yes we run our courses in association with various universities and colleges and we offer a range of courses right the way up to BA Hons and MA levels.'

**Q:** What skills and or qualifications do you want in a teacher?

**A:** 'A guitar department is like a football team. We're not necessarily looking for everything in one person, but over the department we need great CVs with hit record experience, high-level session and touring experience, good reading, theory and transcription abilities, a few hot technical guys, some feel players, at least one jazz and world music specialist.

The best possible thing to get under your belt is high-level recording. People who make hit records think about music in an entirely different way to those who haven't been through that. I wouldn't really be able to use a glorified bedroom player however well they can shred. Today's music students need a bit more than that!'

*Now let's take a look at some of the most common questions I've been asked about working in music retail...*

**Q: What sort of skills do you need to work in a music shop selling guitars?**

**A:** It comes as a surprise to a lot of people that one of the primary skills necessary in this department is the ability to sell and the common sense to make sure that negotiations run smoothly and that all the necessary paperwork is completed, too.

Unfortunately the cliché of the guitar shop salesman is someone who is only too eager to show off and grandstand his skills as a player to the public at large at the drop of a hat – and generally run down, humiliate and denigrate customers at the same time. It also helps if he is brusque, ill-informed, stylistically blinkered, musically illiterate and downright rude, too!

It's a shame that this is the only type of music shop salesperson you hear about – the majority of the conscientious, pleasant, genned-up, helpful and thoroughly nice types barely get a mention. But I think we've probably all experienced poor service in retail stores at one time or another – whether they were musical instrument outlets or carpet shops – and so we can pretty much judge for ourselves what type of person would do well in a career selling guitars.

I've worked in a couple of music stores – in one as shop manager – and so I've seen music retail from both sides of the counter, as it were. I found that a lot of people want to come in merely to talk about instruments – to seek an informed opinion or maybe some advice. So patience and the ability to get along with people are very important qualities here. Also, you'll find that a lot of people will come in, try three different guitars and then leave, having bought a plectrum – but this is all part of the business of building customer relations and without them, the store isn't going to prosper, no matter what kind of six-string eye candy you have hanging on the wall.

If I go into a music store for some strings or some other small item and get treated with respect, courteousness and an air of general friendliness, I'll be far more inclined to go back later on to make a more major purchase – after all, if they've got it right selling the small stuff, I can certainly trust them with the larger more expensive items.

**Q: Can working in a music shop be advantageous if you want to become a professional player, though?**

**A:** Now this is another question. I certainly found that having a basic, ground-level knowledge of how the manufacturing industry worked, gave me a lot of valuable information that I could use in the future. It also gave me access to a lot of different equipment that it would have taken me months to track down and try out.

After all, you can't sell something if you don't know how it works and so part of the job was playing with all the new toys that came into the shop – and this sort of experience helps you form conclusions that will help you make the right choices when selecting gear yourself, a little farther down the road.

Music shops also tend to be meeting places for all the local semipro and pro musicians in the area and, as we know, in the music business contacts are everything. You're often first to get to hear who is hiring – openings in bands and so on – which could lead to joining bigger and better bands as you work your way through the ranks – or pay your dues.

Naturally, you would expect some kind of discount on purchasing your own equipment – maybe even at trade prices – and this can act as an extra incentive to put up with all the questionable renditions of *Smells Like Teen Spirit* you have to endure on a Saturday afternoon!

*And what about getting into Music Journalism?*

**Q:** How do I get to write for a guitar magazine?

**A:** As you can probably imagine, as a former magazine editor myself, I get asked this question quite regularly!

To begin with, the first question that needs asking in return is 'can you write to magazine standards?'. The last thing an editor or sub-editor wants to do is to sit and re-write a piece he's commissioned before it's let loose on the page and so a prospective freelancer is going to have to prove that he or she has got what it takes in the literary stakes before proceeding any further.

Therefore it's quite likely that your first entrée into the world of journalism would be to supply an example of your writing skills so that the editor knows exactly what he's dealing with prior to any commissions being given.

**Q:** So how good is good enough?

**A:** We used to say that A-Level English was the minimum standard, as a rough guide. It doesn't mean that you actually need to have sat and passed the exam, but it gives you at least some idea as to what kind of standard is expected. The next thing an editor will look for is someone who can stay on topic without resorting to cliché or unnecessary waffle. A guitar mag journalist's main task is to entertain and inform the reader and so a factual, gently humorous,

easy-to-read piece is going to win hands down over something that, despite being text book perfect English, is about as interesting as the manual for a washing machine.

**Q:** So how do I go about submitting a piece for perusal by the editor?

**A:** Your first point of contact might be a phone call to the magazine's production editor, just to find out if anyone will actually read something if you send it in. The mag might have a full roster of writers and not actively engaged in recruiting any more. Or they could be frantically busy and just not have the time to talk – magazine deadlines put a lot of stress on an editorial team and someone who wants to give you their life story on the phone when you're trying to get some pages proof read isn't going to be high on the list of prospective freelance writers!

So it might be a good idea to ask if it's convenient to talk – or perhaps there might be a better time? In any case, once you get through to someone, you've probably only got a few minutes to convince them that you're a good investment as new writing talent for the title. Make sure that you know the magazine, its style, its writers, the sort of things they cover, etc – don't go in there blind. This way, you can say that you think you would be good for writing an instrument review or conducting an artist interview – whatever. I would imagine that if you manage to get by an initial phone call, you would probably be invited to submit a piece to the editor – either something previously published (extra brownie points here) or something that you will prepare specially.

Once you have submitted your test piece – along with a CV showing your previous experience, or what kind of forays you've already made into the music industry, you'll play a waiting game. You might need to phone a couple of times to ask if the piece has been read yet, but if you do, remember that the keywords here are patience and politeness. As I've said, editorial teams are busy throughout the publishing month and free time can be scarce – so persistence will pay off, but only if it's accompanied by an understanding of how busy these people really are.

If your test piece is OK, you may be commissioned to write a short piece for inclusion in the magazine – but such a commission will still have the option not to publish if the writing is not up to editorial standards. So it's a hard world to get into and you have to be prepared to work to deadlines and to keep within the confines of your commission at all times.

**Q:** Is it true that you get to keep all the gear you review?

**A:** I thought I'd include this question – something I've been asked often in the past. The short answer is no, we don't. Review stock is sent in by manufacturers, photographed and appraised – and then sent back. The closest we get to deals on gear is being able to buy at a discounted price if something takes our fancy.

**Q:** What are the main advantages to writing for a magazine?

**A:** I can only speak for myself here because I went into writing with my own agenda and I'm certainly not privy to anyone else's.

Working on a magazine taught me how the manufacturing industry works from the inside. It also meant that I was paid to sit there and play with guitars and amplifiers all day!

It taught me how to hone my skills as a writer and introduced me to the rules and regulations of publishing in general – and you can imagine how that has helped me out as a writer of tutors and other books since.

But I think personally, the best part of magazine work was doing interviews as it gave me a chance to meet some of the people I've admired professionally for years. It also placed me in positions I definitely wouldn't have had any access to in my previous incarnation as a guitar teacher. Getting backstage at some of the biggest gigs in the country taught me how the job of playing music is done at the highest professional level – and that's experience you can't buy anywhere else.

Most importantly, it introduced me to a lot of people who have since become friends – and that's invaluable, too!

*Another area of professional music worth considering is playing aboard ship or at a holiday camp. I asked my friend Brian Kettle, whose long career in professional music has seen him cruise the Mediterranean and Caribbean several times, as well as playing in numerous holiday camps across the UK.*

**Q:** How do you get a gig on a cruise ship or holiday camp?

**A:** 'Both the ships and holiday camp gigs are normally accessed through agents and the best place to start looking is on the net. There are lots of websites now that cater for individual musicians finding work and the agents' contact details will be on there, all you need to do is give them a call.

There are also many agencies/cruise lines

that allocate one or two days for auditions and you can find these on the web – and some are even done over the phone.'

## Q: Do you need to know how to read music to play on cruises?

**A:** 'You have to read for this type of gig. If playing cruises is something you want to do and you're not a reader then it's advisable to wait until you have worked on your reading to the extent that you're comfortable with your ability in that direction.

I've seen people fall flat on their faces because they thought that they could ride the gig out or pick it up by ear and there's nothing worse than a bad experience like that. It can put you off playing an instrument altogether, especially when you're young, and so it's best to be ready. It doesn't mean that you're not a good player, it just means that it may not be the right gig for you at this time.'

## Q: What's the cruise ship gig like?

**A:** 'There are two types of band that work the cruise lines. The 'dance band' – who work in one of the lounges, playing music for the passengers to dance to – and the 'show band'.

My experience is more with the show band which works in the on-board theatre pit. The work is varied and interesting, involving backing the cabarets that are flown in, backing shows and playing pre-show music for about 20 minutes every night – jazz mostly. Usually there are two shows a night, each of which lasts for between 45 minutes and one hour. Six nights a week is the average, but I have done a six month contract without a night off at all! It depends on the company and what is expected of you and this can vary enormously.

The shows are normally on 'click track' and, like everything, some are good fun to play whilst others are not so good and

consequently become a bore, especially after a period of time playing the same show.

For cabarets there's normally a band call at around five o' clock when you get to play through the charts – and musicians, being lazy types, like to be in and out of there as soon as possible! This is another reason why a good reading ability is necessary for this type of gig.'

## Q: What sort of artists do you have to back in cabaret?

**A:** 'The cabaret music you'll have to tackle involves a wide range of styles, depending on the type of act you're backing. Vocalists may have big band charts, pop, funk, songs from the shows or just plain swing numbers, but usually they have a smattering of all of it.

Comedians may only have a few tunes in their pad, or just require the band for a play on/play off, which means hopefully a bit of time off stage whilst the act is on, coming back only to play them off at the end.'

## Q: How long do contracts last?

**A:** 'Contracts for the ships can vary in length, but normally they like you to do six months. You may be able to negotiate with the agent – and, of course, once you've done a couple of contracts you might get a call out of the blue asking you to dep for the odd week or whatever due to illness, etc.

The reason why most people want to work on the ships – besides money – is to travel; to see more of the world and to see it for free. It's a great gig for that reason alone and there's no denying that if those things appeal to you, then you'll love it.'

## Q: What's the accommodation on board like?

**A:** 'Normally the only person who gets his own cabin is the MD (musical director) which means that you'll be sharing with someone else in the band. The accommodation is adequate but not palatial and the same goes for the food!

Even though you are a musician, you're considered to be a crew member and therefore you're obliged to take part in the crew and passenger drills. It's no big deal really – there may be one or two per week – but it can become a bit of a drag after a few months. The other thing is that ships, having a regime of safety, may require you to pass a few safety courses before you're entitled to work on board.

The other thing to remember is that, as you'll be sharing a cabin, you need to be able to get on with people – especially the other band members – fairly well. There's not a lot of fun in having arguments or bad feeling with those you live in close proximity with.

Don't let all this put you off though; the plus side far outweighs the negative. There is a good standard of musician doing cruises and if you get on a ship with a really good cooking band, then you'll have a ball.'

**Q:** How does working in a holiday camp differ from a cruise gig – apart from the fact you're not at sea?

**A:** 'These days holiday camps/villages are a similar type of gig to the cruise ships. Shows on click, cabarets, reading, etc – the real difference is that you're only required to play one show per night, but with the addition of two band sets during the course of the evening.'

*If playing for shows takes your fancy, another avenue open to you is to get into pit work, which entails playing in the band in musicals in London's West End, for instance. The work is quite specialised and reasonably hard to break into, but the rewards are high and once your name has become established in the field, you're practically guaranteed work.*

*I asked my friend Phil Hilborne who plays in the West End smash* We Will Rock You *to guide us through the labyrinth of working in a pit orchestra...*

**Q:** How do you get a job playing in a musical?

**A:** 'There are two ways, basically. If it's a new show you can find out who the producers or fixers are from reading magazines like *The Stage* and finding out if they are holding auditions for the band. Sometimes they do, sometimes they just contact people who have worked with them before and who are a known quantity. Some players will call at the theatre and leave tapes of themselves playing with contact information. Or it might be done on personal recommendation by someone who has worked with the fixer or musical director before, can't do it themselves but knows someone who would fit in well and do a good job.

By the way, fixers are the people employed by the show who are responsible for everything that is musician related – and that often includes the selection of musicians and their payments, contracts and so on.

If they do hold auditions then they might tell you to learn a specific song from the show and then you'd go along with a load of other musicians and play in front of the fixer, producers or musical director. Basically the way it goes is you'd sit in with the band, play the song through, they'd say, 'thank you very much...' and you'd go and wait around until they either tell you that they want to see you again or 'thanks but no thanks'. If they do want you to go back for a second audition it would probably be a bit more full-on. You might have to play through some more material from the show with one or two other people from the production present. It varies from musical to musical.

On *We Will Rock You* I understand that the final auditions were held at Roger Taylor's house with Brian May there as well, but that might be an exception, I can't say.

Once the band has been chosen, rehearsed and the musical has opened, after a couple of months – a sort of 'settling in' period where minor adjustments are made to the score and the individual parts – the band members are allowed to call in 'deps' or 'deputies' and these are often guys they know, obviously, as they don't want to put anyone up for the job who is going to fall flat on their faces and let the production down.

When the show is up and running, there might be two or three deps for the main performer so that cover is always available if someone can't do it or wants the night off.'

**Q:** How do they audition deps?

**A:** 'In my case, I went in and watched the show from the pit sitting behind one of the production's two guitarists, Laurie Wisefield, and sort of picked up on what was needed in terms of the actual performance. Then I took a Mini Disc of the show and a copy of the score home with me and sat and learnt it – both on my own and with some invaluable help and guidance from Laurie. When I thought I'd got it down, I called Laurie up and said I was ready to go in for an actual performance. So we fixed up a date and I went in to play with Laurie watching me. They do things this way so that if you screw up, the main guy can take over so that the show isn't sent off track. I've seen it happen – especially with drummers for some reason – the MD comes through in the in-ear monitoring and says; 'Pull him off!' and you go home, never to return. So preparation is everything.

In my case, the first time I did it, it wasn't perfect but it was good enough to show everyone that I could do it and that any rough edges could be smoothed out fairly quickly. I can remember sitting there playing the final chord on 'Bohemian Rhapsody' and thinking, 'Thank God that's over!' But I got another call very shortly afterwards and started depping on my own on a regular basis.

**Q:** Do you have to be able to read music?

**A:** 'Possibly not – it depends on the individual circumstances. Some musicals – the older, more established ones – you could learn from tapes, but it's risky.

The thing is that written notation is the standard language among musicians, and if the MD decides to make any changes or there are any revisions or additions to the score, the chances are that you're just going to be handed a sheet of music and you might not get much of a chance to read through it before show time.

If it's a new musical, you'd probably be in trouble if you couldn't read. Good readers get to work a lot because they get a reputation for being able to go in, play by sight and do a good job.

Once you've played the show a few times you tend to be able to memorise it, but I like to have the score there in front of me as more of a guide than anything else – a sort of safety net. I've got my own copy of the score at *We Will Rock You* with my own personal notes written in the margin and it's certainly comforting seeing it there every night.

On occasion I've forgotten to take my score in and had to read through someone else's and that can be a little scary because I've become so used to seeing my own. In fact, my copy of the score has got a page missing because someone wrote some crossword answers down on that back of one of the pages and accidentally threw it in the bin! I rewrote it by hand and it's still in there.

One thing I would say is to learn the beginnings and endings of all of the pieces because that's when you have to look away from the score and watch the MD for cues or endings. It can be difficult to do both at once and you definitely need to keep an eye on the MD because sometimes there's no count in or anything – it's just the drop of a hand and you begin playing. If you miss it, you've cocked everything up.

There are times, too, when you want to be able to look away from the score because there's some action on stage and you want to feel more of a part of it. This is certainly true of the finale in *We Will Rock You*.'

# Q: What sort of notes do you make for yourself on the score?

**A:** 'Things like drawing a pair of spectacles next to the score at points when you need to watch the MD, things like that. Anything you need to remind yourself of, because you might not play the show for a couple of weeks and when you come back to it, it's easy to forget some of the fine details. So you leave yourself a note.'

# Q: Do you work seven nights a week?

**A:** 'Most musicals have around seven or eight performances a week, including matinées. So it's a full-time job for someone, which is why they call in deps. For instance, if you play the matinée and the evening show then you're working long hours – that would be around six hours solid just sitting there and playing with only a short break in between performances. It's too much for one person and so you might get called in to do the afternoon performance while the main guy does the evening or vice versa.

So, if you are a dep, you might get called in once or twice a week – but this can vary enormously from show to show or even from player to player.'

# Q: Other than playing the score, what else does the job entail?

**A:** 'Just doing the job professionally at all times; turning up on time, playing the show right, getting on with people and going home.

You have to understand what's needed of you, too – and know the difference between what your part needs as opposed to how you would maybe want to play it yourself. In other words, you play it the way they want you to play it and not necessarily employ too much of your own style. There are times in the show when you can 'be yourself' but really you are there to represent the artist's music in a positive, accurate and entertaining way. There's a temptation to overplay because you're having fun and the show is exciting and everything – but that's not what's needed. You need to turn in a consistent performance with no surprises for anyone along the way.

Something else that's required is to be able to play with a click track, which is like a metronome beat you hear over your headset so that a song or piece is the same strict tempo every night. In *We Will Rock You* the show opens with *Innuendo* with Freddie Mercury's recorded vocal and so we have to play against a click for some of that to ensure that everything is in time, otherwise it would get out of sync. You have to be able to watch for cues from the MD and generally keep your wits about you.'

# Q: What does the MD do?

**A:** These are the people (generally keyboard players) who are in complete charge of the performing band; they conduct the whole show and set all the tempos and give you cues and so on. In some shows, if the MD is not nearby, you can see him on a TV monitor – this is the case in *We Will Rock You* as the MD is over the other side of the stage from the guitars.

The way that MDs work varies, as do their tempos and the kind of feel and dynamics they are after from the musicians and the band as a whole. Really good MDs such as Mike Dixon and Elliot Ware on *We Will Rock You* will always encourage musicians especially just prior to offering any criticism. It's a lot better to hear someone say 'I love how you play the show, but there is this one small thing I would like you to change...' than hearing, 'You are not playing such and such right...' Good MDs always mix praise and criticism and make you feel valued as a player. It's a very diplomatic job, really!

*When most people think of a session player, they think of a hired gun – the consummate professional who is skilled in all styles of music and who can go into a studio, provide the producer or band with exactly what they want, leave and move on to the next job. This kind of thumbnail sketch isn't necessarily an inaccurate one, but I thought it would be interesting to hear some contrasting views on the subject, all the same.*

*My own session experience isn't particularly extensive – it's an area of professional music that doesn't really suit my temperament, for some reason. But when people find out that I've done a few sessions in the past, there's always one question at the top of the list...*

**Q:** **How well do you have to be able to read music to play sessions? I find sight-reading really difficult and yet playing by ear is no problem at all. I want to try and get into session work or something like that, but I don't know how good a reader you have to be.**

**A:** I know some players who make a good living from playing sessions whose reading skills are pretty rudimentary – but they are booked for their ability to deliver the goods quickly and efficiently none the less. They respond well to requests to 'play this like Hendrix' or 'play something bluesy here' and the chances are that nothing has been written out for them in advance.

On other jobs, all the parts are written out and reading becomes imperative, but from what I've heard, this kind of session is still comparatively rare in the rock, blues or pop guitar worlds.

If you want to acquire some basic reading skills, try practising your sight reading every day and aim to be able to read a melody line at very least to begin with. Practise using material you don't know, otherwise your ear will kick in and help out. Make sure there's some sort of facility to check your efforts, like a recording of the tune you're trying to read handy. If you persevere you'll find that reading becomes easier and easier after a while.

*Next, here's an excerpt from an interview I did with Rick Derringer, whose session credits include Steely Dan – a band for whom perfection in the studio is merely a starting place...*

**Q:** **What was it like working with Steely Dan?**

**A:** 'They are incredible perfectionists. That's the only way to explain it; it's great being in that company. They used the best of the best musicians and it was great to be made to feel one of the band. Something to be proud of...'

**Q:** **The chord arrangements Becker and Fagen use are not exactly standard changes...**

**A:** 'They aren't. They have charts with pretty much everything written out and sometimes it's challenging, but on the other hand, it's always pretty much just a blues. So the challenge of those charts can put you off from the simple reality that exists there. But they are pretty ornate changes around the blues...'

*Another branch of session playing involves the top-of-line film or record jobs, where you are paid to deliver the goods quickly and efficiently. Understandably, at this level, there are no passengers on a job and only the best need apply. Kenneth Knussen is an old friend of mine who has played on numerous film soundtracks including all three* Lord Of The Rings *movies,* Star Wars Episode One, Braveheart *and* Gangs Of New York. *His instrument is double bass and he spends most of his professional life playing with orchestras, touring around the world. I asked him for the low-down on premium session playing...*

**Q:** Do I need to be able to read music to get into session work?

**A:** 'Simply, yes! Although there are many examples of specialist players being asked to play in a certain style and improvising a part on the spot, for the most part recording sessions cost money and the people who pay the bills want results fast. This means employing musicians who can work quickly and the ability to read music on sight is really part of the job description.'

**Q:** What happens at a session?

**A:** 'Typically, the musicians arrive to find a pad of music on the stand. If it is music for a movie this can be dauntingly thick, and you will return from the tea break to find more parts added to the pile as they are printed out behind the scenes during the course of the day. Initially there will be some brief balance rehearsals and the engineers will come out to adjust mics as required before getting on to the recording proper.

Most film music is timed to fractions of a second to suit the images, so for the most part the players will wear headphones and work to click tracks. Each item to be recorded will be played a number of times, always with the red light on so there is no 'rehearsal' as such.

Some composers/conductors work fairly quickly and need only a few takes on each number. Others can take hours over only a few minutes of music.

It's not always obvious what the conductor wants that is in any way different from the previous take, but you always endeavour to do as you are asked. There will be listening breaks so that the conductor and producer can discuss a recent take and see it with the images.

This is a welcome opportunity to relax, but you must be ready to start at a moment's notice and be at full concentration level straight away.'

**Q:** Are you expected to get your part right first time?

**A:** 'Absolutely. Everybody makes the occasional mistake but you won't last long in the profession if you make a habit of it. Reading music is not a talent; it can be learned by practically anyone who is interested in doing so, just like you learned to read at primary school. As with a lot of things, it just takes regular practice.

Playing in orchestras, you have no choice but to read music regularly so your reading improves with little effort. If you wish to practise sight reading on your own, just get piles of music and spend 15 or 20 minutes a day looking at something new and playing it through slowly enough so that mistakes are minimal – and preferably, use a metronome to keep your timing on track, too. It doesn't matter how slow you play something through to begin with: speed comes with time.'

**Q:** How do I get into session work?

**A:** 'It's mostly by word of mouth. If you work regularly with an orchestra, you will find yourself in a recording studio eventually.

All session players are booked by contractors or 'fixers'. Finding out who they are and dropping them a line might work, but it's probably better to get to know other key players in the business who might pass your name on. Working in the musical theatre scene can be good, too, as there is a crossover of players into the session world.

Of course, in the UK most of the work is centred in London which is where all the major studios are.'

**Q:** Is there much call for steel string or electric guitarists on classical gigs or sessions?

**A:** 'Contemporary composers often write for electric guitars and there are many examples of modern 'classical' music, shows, jingles, films that have violins and cellos working with a group of jazz or rock musicians. You need only listen to an evening of television to hear all sorts of styles and instrumentation going on in TV themes, adverts and background music. Recently I performed in a tour of an opera called *The Knot Garden* by the late British composer, Sir Michael Tippett. This is scored for strings, brass, wind, percussion and harp – plus an electric guitar.'

**Q:** Any golden rules for session work in general?

**A:** 'Basically, if you can play an instrument well and can read well, there is always going to be work. But don't waste anyone's time; if you are not up to the job, your session career will be very brief!'

*Perhaps 'road crew' doesn't quite qualify as being a job playing the guitar – but it's definitely a career alternative that will mean working with bands and, for the upper echelon, touring around the world, too.*

*In order to fill in a few of the blanks here as to what exactly the job of guitar tech entails, I'm including an extract from an interview I did in 1994 with Phil Taylor, who is Pink Floyd's head of backline and personal guitar tech to David Gilmour. I think it illustrates many of the demands put upon a band's support crew during a big show and how finite the knowledge of guitars and amplification, as well as all the peripherals, has to be in order to ensure a smooth passage through the sometimes turbulent waters of 'show-time'. The interview was carried out backstage during the band's tenure at Earl's Court during the 'Division Bell' tour. It was an exacting technical show, as anyone who has seen the DVD 'Pulse' that was filmed there at the time will understand...*

The sheer volume of the staging, lighting equipment and other peripheral paraphernalia needed to sustain a Floyd audience's awe quota at warp factor ten is vast. To transport the lot on daily jaunts between the planet's stadiums is enough to give even the most experienced tour manager a full-bore anxiety attack. At the epicentre of this potential maelstrom sits the quietly calm and imperturbable Phil Taylor, David Gilmour's right-hand man and overseer of the Floyd's backline.

'I've been to every Floyd gig for the last 20 years and not actually seen any of them!' says the permanently backstage bound Mr Taylor. He somehow manages to bring calm to the confusion of touring, nursemaiding 118 flight cases of Floydian backline on and off planes and trucks to help ignite the world's stages – 20 years' experience of all things Pink brought into sharp focus.

'I first started working for the band in 1974,'

he continues. 'They were getting ready for a British tour with *Dark Side Of The Moon* and the first things we did were a few rehearsals where they wrote some new material, which was strange for me, being a bit of a fan in those days. We were in this very small, dirty, dingy rehearsal room in King's Cross – just me and the four members of the band for two or three weeks while they came up with some tracks called 'You Got To Be Crazy' and 'Raving And Drooling' which were re-written and turned into 'Shine On You Crazy Diamond' and some of the stuff off the *Animals* album. So on that tour, these new tracks became the first half of the show while *Dark Side...* was the second and 'Echoes' was the encore.'

**Q:** Obviously the crew in those days was not quite so vast...

**A:** 'It's hard to remember exactly, but I think there were around a dozen or 15 people in the crew in those days. Today the

93

nucleus totals around 80, but of course it involves several hundred people overall with all the drivers, the steel assembly guys [i.e. – the stage construction crew] and various other things. When I first worked for them with that small crew, I looked after Roger, Rick and David [Waters, Wright and Gilmour] and the person who looked after the drums also doubled as one of the quad PA crew. So during the show there was only ever me on stage dealing with all of it.'

**Q:** What was David using in those days, gear-wise?

**A:** 'It was very similar to what he uses now. One of the first jobs I did in the band was to go out and buy him some new Hi-Watt amplifiers. I went down to Hi-Watt in Kingston, saw Dave Reeves and bought two 100-watt heads which are still in David's rack today. He had WEM 4x12 cabinets with Fane Crescendo speakers in, identical to the ones he uses now, and he had a couple of Leslie cabinets for a couple of things on *Dark Side...* He also had some Binson echo units, a couple of EMS Synthis which he used for the sequence on 'On The Run' live on stage every night, and a small pedalboard with a Fuzz-Face, a treble and bass boost, a volume pedal and switching system for the delays.

'He had a black Strat that he always used – I think we would have carried a spare, too – but one of the other first jobs I had to do was to go out and buy two lap steel guitars, for the different tunings needed on 'Great Gig In The Sky' and 'One Of These Days', which was an alternative encore but in the end they opted for 'Echoes'. I went off to Sound City, which was the in place to go in the west of London, and they had two Jedsons, a cream one and a red one – they were about 60 quid each and that's what we bought and that's what he still uses, although we've since changed the pickups. In fact, on this tour we found a Fender lap steel and he's been using that.'

Needless to say, things have become a great deal more sophisticated over the years...

'Well, David's main Strat is basically a USA 57 vintage reissue which we got hold of in 1984. It's fairly stock other than it's been fitted with EMG-SAs, plus an EMG-EXG expander and the SPC midrange presence control. Other than that, apart from the fact that he's had his trem arm shortened, it's pretty much stock. For a spare he's got a virtually identical Strat which we managed to buy. When we were on David's solo tour in 1984, he went into Manny's in New York with Mick Ralphs, who was his second guitarist on the tour, and Mick picked up this red Strat and said it was really nice and that he was going to buy it – but David wished he'd found it first! Then later on I saw this secondhand red Strat in Chandlers which was just like David's, and so I picked it up and said, 'Whose is this?' and they said it was Mick's. So I said, 'Right, we'll have this!'. It needed a fair bit of work done on it and it's been fitted with the EMGs, too.

'I also carry one more spare which is a cream coloured 57 reissue; David's not very fond of the colour, but it's very nice to play. Other guitars he used on the tour were two Telecasters which are both 52 reissues; the only difference between them is that one of them has the bass string tuned to D, which he uses for 'Run Like Hell'. The other one, which is in regular tuning, he uses for 'Astronomy Domine'.'

**Q:** David's acoustic guitars are Gibson J-200 Celebritys...

**A:** 'They made a run of only 90 of these particular guitars in 1984/85 and we've now obtained three. David just really likes them; they sound great and they're really lovely to play. I've had them modified, they've got EMG acoustic pickups in, but they've also got small Crown microphones in them too. So there are basically two outputs from each guitar: two separate radio transmitters on them with two different signals. Then there's a Gibson Chet Atkins electro-classical which he uses on 'High Hopes' and the two steel guitars which we talked about earlier.'

**Q:** So much for the guitars, but from then on in, things become a lot more complex. To look at, Gilmour's rig is pretty intimidating...

**A:** 'The design concept was to achieve a user-friendly system with the cleanest possible audio signal, using the highest quality components between guitar and amp to eliminate hums, buzzes, RF interference, etc. So the electric guitars go into a Pete Cornish routing system, which is basically 24 sends and returns, controlled via a Custom Audio footboard, modified by Pete, with individual on/off switches for all send and return loops plus a microprocessor which calls up preset combinations of effects with MIDI channel change information being sent at the same time. Then a song title display is built in, which works via MIDI, with a duplicate display in the rack.'

**Q:** Phew! So, judging from some of the pedals on top of the rig, one could say that it's a strange marriage of hi and lo tech?

**A:** 'I guess we've taken advantage of technology inasmuch as David has enough to think about up on stage, being the focus of attention, and so his switching system and equipment have to be as simple as possible. At the end of the send and return routing, it then goes into a master unit which, because I have his amp racks backstage with me, has master volume controls on it for Dave to control his 4xl2s, Doppolas and voice box from on stage.'

**Q:** From a gig to gig point of view, it's pretty easy to put in situ and fire up night after night with maybe just a few slight tinkerings.

**A:** 'It is, yeah. There are a few minor tweaks; I always set his gear up so that it sounds good to me and the levels seem right, however the reason why he likes to have his rack on stage with him every night and the reason why his pedals are mounted on the top is so that he can wander over and give them a tweak as he feels necessary. Pete Cornish has modified most of the 'off the shelf' effects units for both correct matching – level, impedance and so on – and has included several 'artistic' mods for improved usability.'

Keeping his boss briefed on the latest equipment isn't the foreboding task it might at first seem...

'Between projects there are often quite long periods where David doesn't play much guitar, but when there is something – a tour or album – about to happen then I keep my eyes open as to what's around and take him stuff to try.'

Next in line is the preamp stage.

'We use an Alembic F2B, mid 70s bass guitar preamp based, I believe, around a Fender Showman circuit, which is very clean and with minimal controls: brightness, volume, middle, treble and bass. It has been modified to reduce the bottom end and fitted with an extra valve. The way in which David uses his system is that he always gets a good, nice, powerful clean sound – a lot of his sounds are basically clean with a bit of delay – and when he does his overdriven stuff, he introduces various pedals. I guess a lot of people these days would look on that as an old-fashioned way of doing things, but he is from the 'old school' where you would have a couple of effects pedals on the floor going into your amp or combo. We continue to try the modern multi-effects units but, although they appear to be improving, there are sounds which David has got on record over the years by using pedals which cannot be duplicated by those units. A lot of them tend to be good or reasonably good, but they're never brilliant.'

**Q:** So much for multi-effects, but whither the Gilmour generated electrons next?

**A:** 'The signal then comes from the preamp and goes into his volume pedal and from there it goes off, splits and goes into his delays. Then it comes out through the master routing unit and goes into his HIWATT

95

power amps. I've got three normal HIWATT heads, APlOOs, which have a preamp in, but Pete Cornish has modified them so that we're just using the power amp stage, just going in using the master volume and the presence control.

'Then there's another rack with the other three which are slave amps. They're all run with Mullard EL34s. One HIWATT powers a WEM 4x12 with the Fane Crescendos in it and a Marshall with Celestions; the second one does the same thing but it has a chorused version of the first signal – in effect, this means that one has a wet signal and the other remains dry. Then we have a spare HIWATT in the rack. In the second rack, the top HIWATT powers his voice box [a Jim Dunlop Heil], but what I did there was get Pete Cornish to make me a dummy load, because what a lot of people have found with heavy voice box usage is, because of the nature of the driver in them, which is a mid-range horn driver, generally they don't work below 800 cycles.'

One unique aspect of Gilmour's stage rig are the Doppolas – custom-built, revolving speakers.

'I designed them in conjunction with a guy called Paul Leader and had them built. What we were trying to do was make a full range, reasonably high-powered rotating speaker unit. We didn't want to use a Leslie, although David has a Leslie simulator in his rack, we wanted a slightly different sound. It has two six inch 100 watt drivers in it, stacked on each other which is a lot of weight to move around, but they seem to work quite well. We have three of them on stage which are used continually in conjunction with the 4xl2s.

'We were influenced by David getting hold of a thing called a Maestro Rover, which is a revolving full range speaker he uses in the studio. They're quite nice, but fairly low powered and so for live work we needed something with more power.'

Phil's showtime position backstage is just behind Gilmour's row of 4xl2s. Conditions are fairly cramped, but workmanlike – here, he has to be able to deal with all the problems that might crop up during a performance. Anything from a simple tune up to major MASH like effects surgery has to be possible. Essential, therefore, is Phil's workstation – quite literally mission control.

'In my workstation I have drawers of strings, spares and all sorts of exciting things. The tuner unit I had custom made for the 94 tour which includes a Peterson 19' strobe tuner and a BOSS TU-12, with some lights and a dimmer so I can see what I'm doing and a switching system so I can send the signal to either a Fender Super Champ or to a headphone amplifier.

'So if I'm tuning an acoustic guitar and I can't really hear, I can just put on a set of headphones, turn the volume up and get on with it. I also have the ability to monitor David's instrument and radio system through the workstation while he's performing, which is my first checkpoint for troubleshooting any problems which crop up. I have headphone monitoring available at key points throughout his system in order to locate any problem quickly.'

There is a constant turnaround of guitars during a Floyd performance and everything has to be pre-tuned and generally spot on.

'Absolutely. Before the show I pull things into tune that are going to be used during the first half of the show, but I spend most of the number before a guitar is needed tuning it. There are always temperature changes which will affect tuning, especially in the outdoor stadiums as you approach nightfall.'

The positioning of Phil's workstation must mean that things can get fairly loud... 'Pretty loud, yeah, but not horrendously so; you can stand by each other and talk. Basically I'm here listening to Dave's system and tuning. I get called up on stage for different reasons, but generally I'm just listening for any of the equipment going wrong. I'm always on red alert!'

**Q:** What sort of things do go wrong?

**A:** 'On this tour we've had to deal with a lot of temperature changes and we've had to set up in the rain a lot because of the number of outdoor venues we've been doing. You set up in the morning and it may be cold and raining and then by afternoon, the sun's come out and it's got really hot so you have to put space blankets on the equipment to keep the sun off. The pyro on stage contributes a lot of dust and filth every night which gets into everything. I've had a few failures; nothing went wrong on the first part of the tour but gradually some of the pedals started not working properly and I had two or three of those go down. Apart from that, the only other thing was one of the radio transmitters failed.'

**Q:** What happens to all the gear during Floyd downtime?

**A:** 'We have a warehouse where I have David's gear set up so that I can play with it, but generally it doesn't get used very often. Elements of it get used, but as an entire system it doesn't because there's nowhere to use it, it's too big. David's studio is on a boat and not very large and so there's just no room to set it up anywhere.'

# 6: SONGWRITING

*Once your guitar playing has progressed to a certain level, you might begin thinking about using your skills creatively and writing some music of your own as a prelude to playing live. Here is a selection of questions relating to the task of modern music making...*

**Q:** I've written some songs – how do I copyright them?

**A:** This always seems a lot more complex than it sounds. A lot of people either write their piece out or record it onto a CD and then mail it to themselves using registered post (i.e. dated and signed for) and then lodge the unopened envelope somewhere safe – either a bank or a solicitor or just somewhere secure in the house.

This way, your song has literally acquired itself a 'date of birth' and in the unlikely event of someone copying it (these cases are comparatively rare) you have proof that your original was around at a certain date and time.

If you've recorded your song onto a commercial CD, then it's a good idea to get in touch with one of the royalty collecting agencies like MCPS (Mechanical Copyright Protection Society, www.mcps.co.uk) and PRS (the Performing Right Society, www.prs.co.uk) and talk to them about registering your work officially.

**Q:** Is there computer software available for writing out music?

**A:** There's an abundance of programmes – the two main contenders used by professional publishers being either Sibelius (www.sibelius.com) or Finale (www.finalemusic.com).

Both sites have downloadable demos of their software available so you can try before you buy.

**Q:** I wondered if you could give me some advice on how to get started as a songwriter. I am a serious guitar player and play classical, rock, blues, pop and can occasionally stray into basic jazz. I have written some material that I feel is very good and has real potential, my problem is I don't know what to do with it next. Where is the best place to send my ideas and in what form should they be, recording/manuscript and what quality?

**A:** If you already have some songs written, it might be an idea to approach a song publisher and try to get your work professionally published. All sorts of advice on this and other matters you mention can be found at the websites like the Mechanical Copyright Protection Service (www.mcps.co.uk) the Performing Rights Society (www.prs.co.uk) the Musicians' Union (www.musiciansunion.org.uk) or the Guild of International Songwriters and Composers (www.songwriters-guild.co.uk) all of which are good places to start.

With regard to quality as far as either demos or manuscript are concerned, if you aim for the best possible, you won't go far wrong.

**Q:** I've come up with some melodies, which I want to accompany on guitar. Can you give me some pointers as to how work out the chords to support them?

**A:** First of all I'd advise you to get hold of a couple of books on harmony as these will cover a lot of the information you need.

A lot of classical composers work in the way that you describe – harmonising a melody – and so the procedure is well documented. The full story is too intricate to go into here, but basically the first task is to identify the scale your melody resides in. In most cases, this will be the major scale as this is easily the most common scale in Western music (I'm assuming here that you aren't composing classical Japanese opera!). Every note of the major scale can be harmonised to produce a chord and, in general terms, most melody notes tend to be the third of the chord.

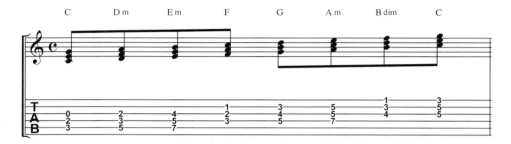

So if we take five notes from the C major scale – to create a 'melody' – we could harmonise it like this:

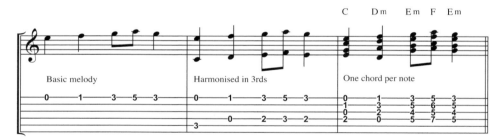

All well and good, but the harmony is too busy; we don't really want one chord for every melody note because it will make everything sound too 'cluttered'. So we can abbreviate the harmony a little and let one chord carry more than one melody note:

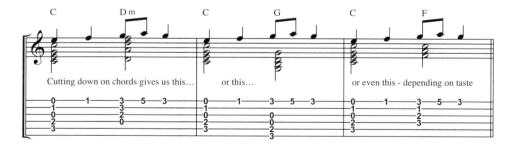

Very basically, as long as the melody notes don't clash with those in the chord itself, this technique will work fine. Sustaining an F melody note over a C major chord won't sound too nice, but changing the chord to an F or D minor will sound fine as both chords contain the note F in any case:

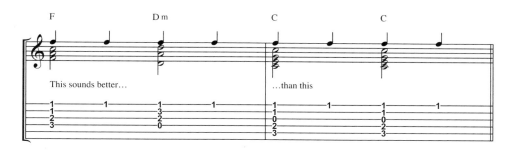

**Q:** I've been trying to work my way through a book that was written for piano, painstakingly working out all the chords on the guitar fretboard, but I find that it's sometimes nearly impossible as the fingerings need a superhuman stretch. Am I right in thinking that piano pieces have to be rearranged for the guitar before they are playable?

**A:** Throughout the guitar's history I think it's true to say that music composed for other instruments has been the hardest to play. In the classical world, it's a well-known fact that Bach's keyboard pieces are notoriously difficult when arranged for the guitar, whereas the music of Villa Lobos, who actually composed on the guitar, is far more logical and fretboard friendly.

It's likely that the guitar suffers from this because of its relatively tiny repertoire when compared to the piano. So little music was actually written for the guitar that we've had to 'borrow' music written for other instruments along the way. It's all to do with the very different way that harmony is realised on the two instruments. Take a look at this, for instance:

It's a perfectly normal C7 chord laid out on the treble clef in the way a pianist might expect to see it (for the right hand) but there's not really a practical fingering for this particular version of the chord on the fretboard. So our versions of C7 tend to look far more like the ones below which both take the guitar's 'fourths tuning' and six string limit into account.

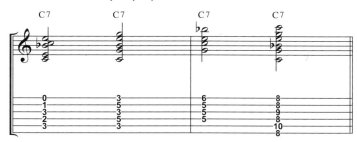

Another of the guitar's shortfalls is close harmony. On the piano, it's obviously very easy to play chords with one or two notes a semitone apart in every key, whereas on the guitar this is a very difficult trick to pull off without retuning or relying on open strings and gargantuan stretches. I suppose piano players can be thankful that they don't have to retune to DADGAD during a concert!

So good luck with your own arranging – I can't help thinking that there must be an easier way, though!

**Q:** What would you suggest for a basic ear training package? I know you've suggested downloading programmes from the net in the past, but none of them really work for me. Where should I start?

**A:** Basic ear training should start with being able to tell major from minor thirds (see below) working up to being able to tell the four basic triads apart. You should also be able to spot the intervals of the major scale – major thirds, fourths, fifths and so on.

The reason why I like the computer programmes so much (I still use one called Pitch Coach 1.1 for Macintosh) is that they can play you intervals, triads and so on completely at random which makes everything easier when it comes to testing the ears. It's difficult to test yourself otherwise.

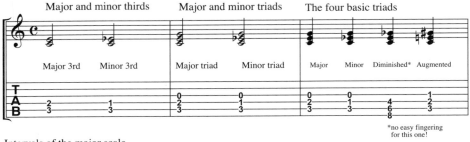

Intervals of the major scale...

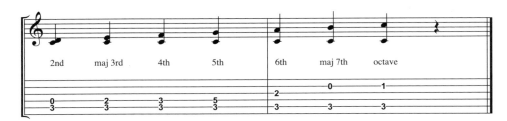

**Q:** I read somewhere in a Joe Satriani interview that he used to play all the chords in a chord book that he had every night and in doing so improved his ear. Do you know which chord book it was and if it would be a good idea for me to do the same? I'm really interested in Joe's playing and anything that would help me get closer to the master's way of thinking would be priceless.

**A:** The chord book concerned was by Joe Pass and was entitled *Joe Pass Guitar Chords* and is available from Mel Bay in the United Sates. Satriani said that after going through each of the chords in the book on a nightly basis for a while he was able to predict the sound of some of them before he heard them and this would have doubtless improved his ear and contributed to his overall sense of music.

Obviously this worked for Joe – but remember that he was also taking music lessons and studying hard and so the time he spent with the Joe Pass book would have augmented his knowledge and not formed it. By all means get hold of the book and follow in Satch's footsteps – it will do your ear good, but whether it turns you into a world-renowned guitar virtuoso is another matter!

**Q:** How on earth do you learn to sing and play at the same time? My first few attempts have caused considerable hilarity among my nearest and dearest, but I'm determined to be capable of turning out at least a half reasonable rendition of a couple of James Taylor songs. Any advice?

**A:** I believe the best way to approach the situation is to learn the melody and accompaniment parts separately at first – and learn them thoroughly, too. So memorise the guitar part so that you can play it through with absolutely no mistakes, pauses or any other glitches.

Once you're at the level where you're playing the accompaniment without having to think about it at all, learn the vocal part without the guitar in your hands. Only when you know both parts so well you could perform them in your sleep, put them together. You'll probably find this tricky to begin with, but practice should iron out any wrinkles still present when you reach this stage.

**Q:** How do I tell which key a song is in? I've got some songbooks and backing tracks, but I always end up trying to play along using trial and error. I know where all the various scales and so on are on my guitar neck, but this is holding me back.

**A:** The definitive way of telling which key a piece is in is by checking out the key signature at the beginning of the music. This isn't completely foolproof, however, as major and minor keys share the same signatures.

The keys of C major and A minor share the same key signature...

... as do G major and E minor

I'm aware that learning all the key signatures by heart takes time – and in my experience there is no alternative to learning them by rote; there aren't any shortcuts that actually work.

There are various checks you can make when looking at a score that will at least offer up some clues as to what key a piece is in, if the key signature still proves too much of a mystery to unravel, though.

To begin with, take a look at the chords above the music – it's quite normal for a piece to end in its 'home key'. So if the final chord of a piece is, say, F major, it would be a good guess that this would be the key of the piece. Check out the final note of the piece, too, as many pieces actually end on the root.

103

The next thing to do is to play the chords of the piece through and see if your ear can pick up on a key centre – is there a chord that sounds like 'home' anywhere in there? If you can detect one of these tonal 'centres of gravity' then it's odds on you've found the right key.

Apart from that, I'm afraid that it's a matter of getting hold of a good theory book and doing some key signature memorisation!

**Q:** I would like to transcribe my exercises or songs quickly. Is there a program that can transcribe what I'm playing directly to my computer?

**A:** I personally use Finale for my music transcriptions (www.codamusic.com). The programme will notate music played into it via a MIDI source so if you equipped your guitar with a suitable MIDI pickup what you are suggesting would be possible.

This is about as close as you can get in terms of having a computer programme take over the tough slog of transcribing for you, but it's got to be said that the transcribers I know all still do it the hard way!

**Q:** I was wondering if you could explain something for me. I was reading a guitar book and came across this sentence: 'The simplest form of chord substitution is that whereby a chord is replaced by one where the root remains the same but the actual type of chord is embellished to produce a different harmonic effect...' Any chance that you could translate this into plain English for me?

**A:** I see what you mean – not the clearest way of putting over the 'simplest' of ideas, eh?

What is meant here is that all major and minor chords begin with three scale tones piled on top of one another (the root, third and fifth, as shown opposite) whilst dominant seventh chords have four notes in their most basic form.

All other chords are formed by adding the remaining scale tones to the basic triads which has the effect of altering their characteristics or 'sound imprints'. In this way, a major sixth or major seventh is still considered to belong to the basic 'major chord family' and so can be seen as a simple substitute for the triad.

In much the same way, dominant ninths, thirteenths and so on can often fit in where the music would call for an ordinary dominant. Naturally, the choice of substitute shouldn't be random as it's possible that the note added to the triad will conflict with the melody note in the song or piece, resulting in a very unmusical clash. But if you play through some simple variations on major, minor and dominant chord forms, you'll soon begin to familiarise yourself with their individual sounds and be able to make an informed choice.

I actually prefer the term 'chord embellishment' when this kind of thinking is applied as I believe it is a better descriptive term – but like I say, the key is experimentation; it's only by employing trial and error that anyone ever finds out what works and what doesn't!

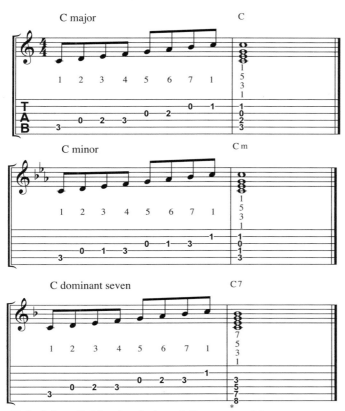

*Seriously impractical fingering - for demonstration purposes only!

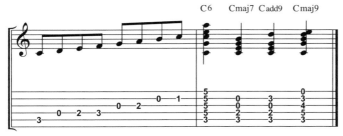

Different combinations of notes from the C scale added to the basic triad offer different textures and can sometimes be substituted for an ordinary C major chord

# 7: JOINING A BAND

*Playing music is essentially a social phenomenon – once you've learned to make music on your own, the next step is to make it with other people. This can involve anything from finding another guitarist to strumming a few songs with a view to joining a band and playing live either locally or nationally.*

*The next section involves questions regarding unleashing your talents on the general public...*

**Q:** I've worked hard on my playing and think that joining a band – or at least playing with other musicians – is probably the next stage in my development. How do I meet like-minded guys who are into the same music as me?

**A:** It's all a question of doing some research and surveying your local music scene. Guitarists tend to be inveterate loners, but there comes a time when you've actually got to get out there and begin making contacts. A good place to start is by visiting the local music shops and asking questions – there might even be a 'sits vac' board in one of them where you can jot down a few phone numbers of local outfits looking for a guitarist.

The other avenue to explore is local music venues – in just about every area there is a pub or club which is the 'hot' place to play, so pay them a visit and get to know the kind of bands on the local scene. The chances are that a lot of the local musicians will hang out there – checking out other bands is all part of the job – and so you might be able to pick up some leads by word of mouth. You might even get to hear about regular 'jam' nights somewhere nearby and this is an ideal opportunity to meet and play with other like-minded people.

Scan the music press on a regular basis – there might be a band in the locale who is advertising for a guitarist. You might even think of placing your own ad, saying that you're looking for a band playing a particular type of music (you can't afford to be too narrow minded here, though) and that could lead to something, too.

Basically, as ever, it's all down to communication; any musician will tell you that it's no good sitting at home waiting for the phone to ring, you really have to get out there and let people know you exist!

**Q:** How do I know when I'm good enough to join a band?

**A:** By going out and watching other bands in your area. That's a good way to assess what sort of level other musicians are at, in any case. But I'll add something here – most guitarists I've taught never think they're good enough to join a band and always need some gentle pushing to take those all-important first steps. I've coaxed some white-knuckled first timers through their debut gigs and they've all ended up loving being on stage. In many cases it's actually more to do with confidence than actual chops.

**Q:** Is it best to join a band where everyone is into the same kind of music or should I think about broadening my horizons a bit and join a band that covers a wide stylistic area?

**A:** Basically, you need to gain some experience first and foremost. You need to know exactly what it's like to be out on stage in front of an audience and how to deal with everything that comes with the job. That experience can be gained anywhere, playing practically anything. In fact, a lot of people I know started off playing in bands where they didn't necessarily like the material overmuch, but they acknowledge that they were 'paying their dues' and that what they learned has proved invaluable ever since.

It's only after a while that your own strengths as a player begin to show through – and they might surprise you, too. Every night you walk out on stage helps you to refine your choice of style and so I'd say that the most important thing is to get in a band – any band – and get out there.

**Q:** I'm looking to join a band at the moment and have been wondering if my gear is up to scratch. I've got a good guitar, some footpedals and a 50 watt amp – am I equipped?

**A:** It very much depends on the band and what sort of gigs you're looking at doing. Hard rock or metal bands might require something a little more blood-curdling in the amplification stakes, but a lot of club or pub bands wouldn't be put off by 50 watts of guitar thrust behind them.

**Q:** I answered an ad in the paper to join a band, but when I met them, it was clear that they are on an entirely different level of competency to me. I don't want to make a fool of myself – what should I do?

**A:** If it's obvious from the start that you're completely incompatible, then it's much better to make some polite excuses and decline any offers to join the band. Forget about it and move on.

**Q:** I really want to play lead guitar, but there's a local group who need a rhythm guitarist – is it worth me checking it out just for the experience?

**A:** It might be – it would depend on what you've already done in terms of playing in bands. If this is your first outing then it

probably would be worthwhile, just to get some hands-on education in live music-making. Otherwise, if you've already built up a creditable CV as a lead guitarist it could be seen as a backwards step. It all depends on the band – if they have a higher profile than you've previously experienced or tend to play bigger venues, then there still might be some worth in considering it. After all, there's nothing wrong with being a good rhythm guitarist – players like AC/DC's Malcolm Young and The Stones' Keith Richards have made an amazing career out of it!

**Q:** What about tribute bands – are they worth joining?

**A:** On the whole, I'd say it's as good an opportunity as any other – and possibly better, depending on the band. I've seen some very, very good tribute bands – and I've seen some that amounted to being nothing more than a Karaoke nightmare in hell!

The advantage of joining a tribute band is that you are practically guaranteed that your audience will turn up knowing exactly what to expect – something that you don't normally experience with run-of-mill pub and club bands. Deciding on material would be an easy job, too as all you really have to do is refer to the latest set lists of whichever band you're basing yourselves upon.

What's more, if the job is done right and the outfit is run along professional lines, you could find yourself playing large venues to capacity crowds – and that ranks as a success on anyone's terms.

Bands like the Bootleg Beatles, Illegal Eagles, Australian Pink Floyd and Counterfeit Stones have achieved some amazing acclaim for the shows they put on – and, watching them perform, you can see the hard work and dedication that has gone into getting the sound of the various songs dead right.

So if you're happy that the band concerned are sincere about doing a really fine job – go for it!

**Q:** I've recently joined a band as 'second guitarist', the idea being that they want the guitar sound to be bigger in the tradition of classic twin guitar outfits like AC/DC. How do I do this?

**A:** Angus and Malcolm Young have the knack for combining two parts so that they sound like one massive guitar – and it's not really as difficult as it might seem. To begin with, Malcolm favours first position open string chords, whereas you'll find his brother's part often residing further up the fretboard and employing barre versions of the same chords.

This is a very good basic plan to adopt for rhythm parts or chordal riffs because it really will thicken the sound up a treat. For example, if we took a perfectly ordinary C maj chord in the first position, omitting the third if you're using a fair amount of distortion and want to keep things from sounding too cluttered, then you'll play something like this:

If your colleague then plays C major as a barre chord on the eighth fret, he'll be playing this:

Practise both chords together until you're absolutely sure that you're playing the exact same rhythm and you'll end up with a huge C chord which will really fill out the sound.

Another idea would be for one of you to play an arpeggiated rhythm part whilst the other bolsters things up with some punctuating chordal fills – think of what's going on at the beginning of AC/DC's 'Hell's Bells', for instance.

In theory, this kind of thinking will help you out most of the time where chord parts are concerned, but riffs are another matter. For these, you can try a similar idea, which would be to play them an octave apart, but this sound won't always suit.

Another idea would be to work out a counter part to the riff – a sort of accompanying rhythm part to fill things out in the lower register or try merely punctuating what's going on with the occasional chordal stab.

Then, there's the whole question of playing riffs in harmony – this is more difficult to work out and will take a fair amount of trial and error, but the result is generally worthwhile.

Melody parts are usually harmonised in thirds and so, if you take the C major scale and one of you plays it from root to root whilst the other plays E to E (see below) you'll find the results very satisfying indeed.

*I get a lot of questions from guitarists who want to start their own bands and run them professionally.*

*To find out what's involved, I turned to my friend Slim from The Hamsters – a band who have spent the last 20 years pounding the highways and byways of Europe clocking up an amazing number of gigs – just under 4,000 at last count, if I recall.*

*The Hamsters' schedule is a hectic one – check out their website at www.thehamsters.co.uk to see how busy they are as a band – and their reputation is such that audiences are bowled over wherever they perform.*

**Q: What's the biggest misconception about running a band?**

**A:** 'That it's glamorous! A lot of people think that it's all about going to parties, generally hanging out and having a good time and being adored – but it's not. The Hamsters do everything themselves – which is unusual – we look after all the various angles of keeping the band running, and it's hard work– very hard work. We did gigs five nights a week when we first started and it was years before things took off.

Running a band is all about finding a balance between being entertaining on stage and administering to the work involved behind the scenes, just letting people know that you're out there. You could be the best band in the world, but if nobody knows anything about you then you're wasting your time.

The level of awareness for us out there on our circuit when we started was non-existent, and it was down to us to turn that around. It was necessary in the first place to write an intriguing biog and have a decent press picture that would get printed and make people want to come and see us. It was also necessary to have a decent demo that would get us work, too.

I never leave promotion to the promoter alone: I always offer as much support as I can because it's a tough job letting people know that a gig is happening, especially when the audience is older and a fragmented social group. For example, we don't appeal solely to students, where all you have to do to let them know is put up a poster in the college bar, so a lot more effort is involved in reaching our fans as they may not go out that much.

You can't just expect people to turn up – no matter what sort of a reputation you think you've built up for yourself. There are many other forms of entertainment that are available to potential audience members these days, and you have to compete with those to ensure that people are going to spend their hard-earned cash on coming to watch you, and not staying at home and renting a movie.

There are bands who have a roadie each and staff doing everything for them, and the band members never become involved in running their operation hands-on. They usually end up having to go back to filling shelves at Tesco's, all the while complaining that they never earned any money and were supposedly ripped off, but if you spend more than you earn being pampered and fabulous, then that's going to happen. They get into it for the assumed glamour and probably because they love themselves a little too much and miss out on the fact that it's still a job of work, when it all comes down to it.

Up until recently, we used to share rooms in hotels, and we still lug our own gear (except when there are stairs!) and really work hard to make sure that we end up keeping most of the money we earn.

You've got to free yourself from any illusions: I was asked by a promoter recently what sort of rider we wanted at a particular gig and I said 'nothing – just a cup of tea or coffee when we get there and we'll be fine'. If we need to feed ourselves then there's always a kebab shop or curry house open and we'll sort ourselves out, rather than being hit for £100 off the top of the split for a rider that we didn't need. Bands love to walk into their dressing room and see a large spread (it makes them feel really important) but if it's you that's paying for it in the end, do you really need it?

It's really all about having no pretensions; do the job and keep as much of the money you've earned as possible without frittering it away on unnecessary items just because you want to feel pampered or special.

It's certainly not enough just to be a good musician, you've got to keep both feet on the ground and a firm grip on the business side of things – the day-to-day running and administration of the band – otherwise it probably won't last.'

**Q: What sort of mistakes are the easiest to make?**

**A:** 'That it's going to be easy, for a start: musicians never want to hear the phrase 'hard work'. It's all very well for pop stars to get drunk, throw a tantrum on stage and walk off halfway through a gig because something's upset them or questioned the image they have of themselves or something.

It's OK, because they've got a record company budget that can smooth things over with the fans and the press via an expensive publicist or spokesman. It's all come too easy for them – they haven't worked for it so don't appreciate it, and think that the show is all about them, but it's not, it's all about the audience. It's about having respect for them and putting on a good show, no matter how ill you're feeling or how pissed off with the world you happen to be that night. Your job is to help the audience forget their worries for the couple of hours that you're on stage – not dump your insecurities on them. The jazz drummer and bandleader Buddy Rich used to tell his musicians, 'don't take your troubles on stage...' and I think that's dead right. Leave them in the dressing room – you can pick them up later.

I heard an interview with Gene Simmons from Kiss some years ago and the guy interviewing him asked what the most important thing was for him at a gig and he said, 'the audience...'. It really surprised the interviewer because a band like Kiss don't necessarily look like they've got their priorities in that kind of order. But it's so true; you're there to put on a show to the best of your ability and if that means getting up there and forgetting about your own troubles for a couple of hours, then that's what you've got to do.'

**Q: Do you use an agent or do you get the gigs yourself?**

**A:** 'We do virtually everything ourselves. I think we've done around 3,750 gigs so far and perhaps only ten or 15 of them were done via an agent. The thing is that we were already 'grown ups' when we started out – we weren't a bunch of kids with an unreasonable grip on reality – we were older, and that helped keep things together.

If you use an agent, you're handing over 10–15% of your fee – for what? If your fee is £2500 for playing somewhere, that means you'd be handing over up to £375 to someone just for making a phone call and sending a contract and posters out. £375 for that? I don't think so...

If a promoter always uses agencies and needs to get in touch with a particular band, or they have a style of music they want covered, then yes, it's worth having your name down with an agent or two for those occasions. Or if a double glazing company want an ABBA tribute band for a corporate event, then they'll probably use an agent for the whole production and want contracts, etc, as they're not used to working in our field.

But these days, thanks to the internet, it's easier to find bands and so sometimes it's actually quicker – and cheaper – to use Google, find the website and deal with the band directly.'

**Q:** What about publicity?

**A:** 'Try to help the promoter as much as you can and certainly don't leave everything up to him alone. We still try to speak to local press and radio because we can talk with authority about ourselves.

The chances are that the promoter has got five gigs happening in the same area at roughly the same time and you need to make sure that you get in on the publicity because the promoter will put the majority of his effort into the show that needs the most help, and that may not be yours! Even if you're quite a high profile band, there's no guarantee that people will know you're playing in their area – and yet the promoter might think that your band's appearance somewhere will take care of itself and spend all his time promoting a much smaller, lesser known act because he thinks that they need it more.

It's only by staying on top of things that you can expect to have people showing up where you're playing. Basically, sticking a poster up at a venue the weekend before you're due to play there isn't good enough – it needs to be two to three months in advance. Flyers, leaflets and so on are great but they need to be out there well in advance to let people know that you're going to be playing. A good promoter will create a vibe months in advance so that your upcoming gig is the one people will be talking about. Even after 20 years, when you're relatively well known, it's a mistake to assume that everyone who wants to come to a gig will know that it's happening – they won't, unless someone or something tells them it is.

Also, publicity has to be done mainly at a local level – national ads are the icing on the cake if your budget will stretch to that. Get in touch with the local papers and see if they'll do an article, and contact local radio too. The commercial stations in the UK tend only to help if you pay for it; the local BBC Radio stations are often very helpful, but they tend not to have as many listeners that rock'n'roll!

We also find that having a website (www.thehamsters.co.uk) and a mailing list is utterly essential. We recently had to cancel a run of gigs as I was sick with a cold, and we whacked out 20,000 emails at a stroke to warn fans that the gigs were cancelled.

These days, it's a good idea to have a MySpace site too (www.myspace.com /thehamstersuk), which helps build a sense of community with your fanbase.'

**Q:** What advice would you give someone who was looking to run a full-time band?

**A:** 'Be prepared. Remember that when you're not out there playing, you're in the office – you're administering the band. It's a full-time, seven days a week job and you do what you have to do, at the risk of it wrecking your personal life too, in some cases.

You have to take the role of a player/manager – not two things that necessarily go together too well, as most musicians are dreamers, not administrators – but you'll find it's necessary to be part musician, part accountant!

The best thing to do is to split the many tasks involved in running a band between the individual members. You literally split the work according to speciality – if someone in the band is good at doing a particular thing, then let him do it. It makes you responsible to each other – you can have regular meetings and keep a check on what's happening and chase each other up if necessary. It doesn't come easy, in some cases, but it's got to be done.'

**Q:** What about merchandising?

**A:** 'It's important, as it helps you run the band from a financial point of view. If you're selling CDs, DVDs and t-shirts at a gig, people will buy them if they like you – but it's important to keep your sense of perspective here, too. If I see someone at one of our gigs wearing a t-shirt with the band's name on it, I always stop and say hi or give them a wave because it's an honour to have someone like the band so much that they want to spend their money to tell the world about it by wearing your name on their chest. It's great advertising, sure, but it's also a great compliment. I get emails from people telling me that while they were on holiday in Yugoslavia or somewhere they met someone wearing a Hamsters t-shirt and ended up having a conversation about the band, which is really a great thing and a fantastic honour. It's a community, more than anything, I guess.

When we play somewhere, we tend to turn up in the afternoon, play the gig and leave – we don't get a lot of time to hang around in any one place, and so it's hard to sum up what people really feel about us. If people want to buy your CDs or t-shirts, then that's giving you some essential feedback, as well as providing another important source of revenue for the band.'

**Q:** Do you need the same level of commitment to run a semipro band, though?

**A:** Not exactly the same level, no – although, in my experience, commitment is still one of the biggest problems you'll have to face. Getting hold of three or four like-minded individuals who are willing to give up some of their precious leisure time to indulge in what is, in effect, a hobby is a lot harder than you might think. If other band members have young families, homes to run, partners to think about then there are bound to be times when rehearsals are cancelled or gigs just not possible because one of you has something to do – a family commitment that just can't be put off.

Apart from that, despite the fact we've dropped a gear from talking about professional music in Slim's answers in the previous section, much of the actual work in running a band remains the same – or at least very similar. In order to work, say, every weekend, you are still going to have to tout

for gigs, do all the legwork necessary to promote the band, make calls and so on. The band is still going to have to rehearse, too, and if the gigs are further apart, you might find that rehearsals have to be more frequent just to keep an edge on the material. It's surprisingly easy to forget chord arrangements, beginnings, endings and so on if they are not frequently bashed out!

**Q:** How do I find out what to charge for hiring my band?

**A:** Ask around. If you ask a few other similar bands in your area, you'll soon be able to see an average. Of course, some bands are inclined to exaggerate a little when asked this question by someone who is a contemporary (and a possible competitor) but asking a cross section should give you a good idea.

Failing this, you could always check with the Musicians' Union (www.musiciansunion.org.uk), who have a 'minimum gig rate', and draw your own conclusions from that.

Once you get established, you can adjust your gig rate accordingly – it's pretty much the same case of supply and demand as exists in any business. My friend and colleague Phil Hilborne tells me that he used to have two prices he would give a prospective customer – one for a bare minimum set with no lights and very few frills, and another for the full-on show.

Offering a choice like this would suit most people as it gives them some control over the situation – and most of them would apparently opt for the more expensive option in any case! But, if you find a smaller concern who want to book you but it's a smaller venue then having the lower price bracket available was appreciated, too.

**Q:** Is it worth registering with an agent?

**A:** It depends on what sort of gigs you want to do. As Slim from The Hamsters said a couple of paragraphs ago, you might feel that you want to take care of this side of things yourself and not have to pay an agent a percentage of your fee. On the other hand, if you want to think about doing some 'functions' – like conferences, corporate dinner dances or the like – then it's likely that an agent will be able to get you some work.

I used to work through an agent to do some gigs – but not by any means all of them. The agreement we had was that I fixed a price for myself and the band and the agent put his fee on top. This way, I ended up with the money I thought was right for the job and the customer paid the agent – which made me feel a lot better! Agents work almost exclusively with contracts and will quite likely negotiate you quite a good deal in the process. If I was doing an 'agency gig' it usually meant that we got some sort of 'refreshments' thrown in during the evening, which varied from a mug of tea and a plate of sandwiches in the venue's kitchen to a full á la carte meal at a table reserved for the band.

# 8: THE MAJOR LEAGUE

*In this chapter, I hope to answer two basic questions – what actually goes on at a 'big' audition and what's it like playing and touring with a name band? In order to address both at the same time, I've called upon some interviews I've done over the past 14 years with players who have had the opportunity to play with some of the biggest bands in the world. Obviously, this is professional music at the highest level, but I think a lot can be learned via reading about these players' very different experiences...*

## 1. Darryl Stuermer
Genesis/Phil Collins

Genesis took a rather unique way round the problem of replacing lost manpower by resolving to confine the writing and recording duties to the surviving three band members and taking on 'extra hands' for live performance. Thus, Milwaukee-based guitarist Daryl Stuermer became a fully paid-up member of the Genesis live auxiliaries...

'Someone else who had auditioned for Genesis and didn't get it actually recommended me. So I got a call one day, saying they would fly me to New York and Mike Rutherford would audition me there.

They had sent me a tape of four songs; one was called 'Down And Out' and 'Squonk' was another. I just brought my guitar, played a couple of minutes of each song and Mike Rutherford said, 'That will be fine. I think you're the one.' And I thought 'I didn't do anything!'

He told me they had auditioned a lot of people back home and that they had five names in America that they were auditioning, and I was the first that day. He said, 'I'll give you a call at around 5 or 6 o'clock at your hotel... I just have to audition the other four, but I think you're the one.'

I think it was after we'd talked a bit and then played a bit our personalities seemed to go well together and our playing did as well. But I was very surprised. I had gone through auditions before and they were much tougher than that. But Mike is a very intuitive and instinctive person and I think that's what he went on.'

**Q:** What was the first thing you did with the band?

**A:** 'It was a world tour! When I auditioned with Mike, he gave me a list of 25 songs to work on and I thought I had to learn them all in five days, because we were starting rehearsals only a week later!

So I got back home and took five songs a day and learned them. I was frantically doing this and I showed up at rehearsal thinking they were going to do all the songs, but we didn't do anything until two or three days later!

It was mainly equipment setting up, and then when we did rehearse we only did a couple of songs a day.'

**Q:** Were the rehearsals in England?

**A:** 'This time we rehearsed in England for three weeks and then flew to Houston, Texas, and rehearsed in the Goodyear Blimp hangar, because the screens the band use are so huge that we had to find a place big enough hold them!

We rehearsed there for about two weeks – it was about 90 degrees in there.'

## 2. David Rhodes
### Peter Gabriel's Band

'In my last year at college I met up with a guy who was an English teacher and we decided to do this kind of 'noise' group, with tape machines and me scratching away at a guitar and him playing Stylophone. We did a series of performances at a theatre in Rotherhithe and only 24 people came, so it was then that we decided to do songs! So we started using backing tapes – we were amongst the first to be doing that, I think. But we were a lot more rock'n'roll than electronic, so we kind of missed out.'

**Q:** So when were you trying to put this band together?

**A:** 'That would be '79. We were using the old Roland rhythm machines, using Latin rhythms, that kind of thing...'

**Q:** What were you playing in those days?

**A:** 'I was trying to play guitar,' he jests. 'I had a Strat for a little while, then I had to sell it.'

**Q:** What was the band called?

**A:** 'We were called Random Hold. We were good at something – I'm not sure exactly what. It was quite crude, but there was some nice stuff – really effective. It was very intense, what we did, and consequently nobody bought the record when it came out.'

**Q:** So Peter Gabriel saw you with Random Hold?

'Yes. He came to see the band down at the Rock Garden, along with all of his management people. By the time Peter saw us, we were just a kind of straight-ahead band. He'd been recommended by a painter called Graham Dean who'd seen us a couple of times up in Oxford.

Peter was looking for a band to work with for the third album. His first record had been made with American session players and the second one was pretty much with his live band with a couple of additions.

He came and saw us then invited us to go and do some demos with him. I was so nervous – I had tummy ache for the three or four days that we were there. I just ate mushy bananas and yoghurt.'

Not very rock'n'roll!

'No, but it stopped me from dying of belly-ache!'

That's a really sad story.

'Pathetic! The funny thing was when we went down there I think Peter was 28 and I must have been 22, and I thought, 'What's this old geezer trying to do?' And it's funny... we're still at it!'

**Q:** Presumably Peter's reputation had preceded him...

'Yes, but I was never a Genesis fan. I once had a girlfriend who forced me to listen to 'Foxtrot', and the only track I liked on that was called Armageddon In 5/4 *(in fact, Apocalypse is In 9/8 – DM)*. Peter asked me at one time if I ever listened to Genesis, and I said no, but the only track I ever liked was this thing in 7/4, and I think it was the only track on that record that he didn't like!'

## 3. Dominic Miller
### Sting's Band

By the time Dominic Miller received the news that Sting was auditioning, he had already made a mark on the UK session scene, having played on albums by Julia Fordham and Phil Collins. He arrived for the audition and entered the rehearsal area, jet-lagged and unaccountably nervous...

'I always thought The Police were quite good, although I didn't have any of their albums, and I knew Sting was a bit of a jazzer, so I reckoned that there was no way I could keep up with that and that I wouldn't get the job. The audition was really funny, and the funniest thing was that I was really nervous – tired out, and completely shitting myself. I turned up carrying my pedal board in a bin liner – really tacky, and all the roadies were very amused.

So I got up on the rehearsal platform, plugged myself in, and I wasn't getting any sound whatsoever, which made me even more nervous. All this time Sting's just standing there being cool, and I'm not being cool.

All the roadies were looking at the amp and rushing around, like they do, trying to find the fault. They checked all the plugs and leads, they even changed the valves on the amp, but they still can't work out what the problem is. Finally, one of them comes up to me, reaches out towards my guitar and simply turns the volume up – and it works! At that point, I thought, 'Okay, I've blown it. It doesn't matter what happens now...'

Next, Sting asked if I knew a song called 'Fragile' – I didn't. I said 'Is it one of yours?' by which point all the roadies were in fits of hysterics. I'm blushing and I'm sweating – it's like I'm in a sauna. So Sting plays it, and instantly I'm home – it's a sort of Brazilian thing which I've played all my life. He asked if I could play it, and so I did, and it came pretty naturally and it was really no big deal.

We played that for about 15 minutes and then we stopped and had a coffee break. Sting says to me, 'Do you want to do the gig?' I said 'Well, yes!' And it just didn't register at all. I was just sitting there normally and saying, 'Er... thank you!'

Then his managers come in and I'm still really not there at all. I'm still sweating from this terrible nervousness and from being such a prat. Then suddenly everyone's taking my phone number, and it all looks very important and rock'n'roll and high-powered. Then I go round to his house and we go out to dinner...'

## 4. Jennifer Batten
## Michael Jackson's Band

Michael Jackson's mid 1990s touring band comprised two guitarists, a bass player, a drummer and two keyboard players. They travelled around Europe by bus – although at the beginning of the 'History' tour the gigs were so far apart that Jackson hired a private plane to transport the band between gigs in places like Taipei and Bombay. But the tour was far from the usual plane, hotel, venue, hotel, plane format; the itinerary allowed for around only two gigs a week and so things were far more relaxed than normal for a globe-trotting rock outfit.

Jennifer had been playing in Michael Jackson's touring band for ten years – although all the audience usually saw of her was a brief appearance up front with Jackson during the solo to 'Beat It' where she played Eddie Van Halen's original solo from the 'Thriller' album note-for-note. 'Every night I go out there and try to get it as perfect as I can, but there's always some little challenge like a harmonic doesn't pop out right or whatever, but that's my 16 bars of excitement in the show...'

On past tours Jennifer was dressed up for the 'Beat It' solo with flashing lights and a dragon costume, but on this tour... 'It's worse! Well, it's worse and it's better. It used to take two and a half hours to get me looking the way they wanted for the show, but now I have a wig that's attached to a leather face mask, so it looks really hard-core but it only takes a couple of minutes to get me ready.'

**Q:** Whose idea was the leather face mask?

**A:** 'It was Michael's...'

**Q:** It seems like the current Jackson tour has been going on for ever...

**A:** 'Exactly. The first thing we did was the 'Dangerous' show for the King of Brunei's 50th birthday in July and then we came back to rehearse for the History tour and flew out to Prague on the first of September. We did all of Eastern Europe, Australia and Japan, took a couple of months break and then came over to Europe for four months. And we're meant to be going to South Africa after this... They said that the tour was going to last two years, but I think it will end up being less than a year and a half in total.'

**Q:** What sort of form do the rehearsals take for a tour as elaborate and theatrical as this?

**A:** 'You know, life is a blur once rehearsals start. I just remember the first tour was a solid month of the band in one room, the singers in another and the dancers in another... The second month was full production with pyro and Michael and everything together on a huge sound-stage. This time I know it wasn't two months total – but it was maybe three weeks each.'

**Q:** So Michael gets involved about half way through rehearsals?

**A:** 'Yeah – which means he doesn't have to sit there while we learn how 'Billie Jean' goes...'

**4.** Mike Keneally
Frank Zappa's Band

A lifelong Zappa fan, guitarist Mike Keneally was a regular caller to the Zappa information line, '818 Pumpkin'. When he heard that Frank was preparing to tour, he took the opportunity to call Zappa's office, to offer his services.

'I said 'My name's Mike Keneally and I sing and play guitar and keyboards and I'm familiar with everything Frank has done...' They said they would pass the message on, but they didn't know if Frank was looking for anyone just then. I kind of figured that was the end of it, but I was very surprised to get a call the next day asking if I would come up that evening for an audition.

I couldn't go that night as I had a gig in San Diego, so I asked the woman at the office if it would be possible to audition on Sunday. She wasn't sure if Frank was auditioning on Sunday and told me that she would get back to me, and I hung up figuring that I had made a terrible error.

I went to the club that night where we were supposed to be playing and found that there was another band's equipment on the stage – the club owner had hired another group, and hadn't called me to tell me about it! So not only did I fritter away my Zappa audition, but I also didn't have a gig. That was the low point of my existence...

But fortunately the following Saturday afternoon I got a call from Frank saying 'I understand you know everything I've ever done...' and I said 'Yeah, I'm definitely familiar with it all,' and he said 'Do you have any idea how many songs that is?' and I said 'Well yes; they're all in the other room' and Frank said 'I don't believe you. Get your ass up here and prove it to me!'

So I had my brother drive me up while I practised guitar in the back seat, and since I was playing in the car anyway I didn't bother putting the guitar in a case. I just walked in with the guitar in my hands, and the first thing Frank said when he saw me was; 'Nice case...'

He had told me to learn 'Sinister Footwear 2' and 'What's New In Baltimore?', and I plugged in and played those for him well enough to demonstrate that I was familiar with the repertoire.

Then he just started naming songs to see whether I was full of it or not, regarding my depth of knowledge of his work.

At the end he just said 'Come back on Monday so that the rest of my band can witness your particular splendour!''

## 5. Tim Renwick
Pink Floyd

'I go way back with Floyd because I was at school in Cambridge – the Cambridgeshire County High School for Boys – with Storm Thorgersen, Syd Barrett and Roger Waters. In actual fact, Syd Barrett was my patrol leader in the school scout troop! I knew of Dave as a guitarist very early on, he was in a band called Jokers Wild, who used to do all the university functions, May Balls and stuff like that. Dave was a bit of a hero of mine, in fact.

I kept in touch with him through Willie Wilson who's the drummer with The Sutherland Brothers and Quiver, a very good friend of his. Dave used to help out the Sutherlands quite a lot and we used his home studios to do demos on occasions and he produced a couple of B-sides for us. He used to come and jam with us but I've never actually worked with him in any other way as a formal second guitarist. I did do some odd bits for the Floyd and also there were a lot of other points of contact because the Sutherlands' manager was Steve O'Rourke who manages Floyd, so he put us on shows with them as well. When they came to re-record some of the tracks for the film soundtrack of 'The Wall', Dave asked me to go in and play a couple of acoustic things... so yeah; we go back quite a long way.'

**Q:** So it was more of a natural progression to be asked to join the live touring band?

**A:** 'I was quite surprised to be asked, in fact. At that time I didn't really believe that the Floyd would be going back on the road – it had been seven years or something and there was all this pending legal stuff. So when David mentioned it to me I didn't think I should take it seriously. Originally it was just going to be a tour of America, but the moment the tickets went on sale, three nights in Toronto sold out in a matter of hours and it just snowballed from there.'

**Q:** Any show which involves so many 'moving parts' usually calls for some fairly intense production rehearsals, but in Floyd's case...

**A:** 'We had two weeks, although it was quite condensed. We were in a rehearsal studio in London where we had the whole backline set up as it would be on stage, essentially bashing through the set a couple of times and just working on little bits and pieces. In fact, the first week David was finishing off mixing 'Division Bell' anyway so I was given the job of MD. We had a long list of old stuff to go through as well as the new album, so when David turned up we could play something in excess of 30 songs.'

# 9: REHEARSING

*Once you've got yourself into a band, or a duo, trio or whatever – some form of music combo – you'll need to think about rehearsing. There's a distinction to observe here that I think a lot of players miss – and that is the fact that 'rehearsing' is different from 'practising'. The distinction is that by the time you get together to rehearse some repertoire material, all the practising should be done. In other words, all the individual parts of the ensemble should be up and running and rehearsal is really the time when you blend everything together into a performance.*

*You might want to re-read that paragraph a couple of times...*

**Q:** We desperately need somewhere to rehearse – what kind of venue should we approach?

**A:** Begin looking around the local music shops and see if there are any places advertising on bulletin boards.

Ask guys from other bands where they rehearse, too, as you can often find somewhere suitable by word of mouth alone.

Failing that, try the usual suspects: scout huts, village halls, back rooms in pubs, outhouses, dance halls – literally anywhere that has the space but isn't in the middle of a quiet residential area where noise during unsocial hours could be a problem.

If you live in a city, the chances are that a last resort would be a custom made rehearsal space, which would probably prove more expensive than the local village hall, but enjoy the benefits of being 'acoustically appropriate' to your needs and would probably have musician-friendly facilities like coffee machines and pool tables, too.

**Q:** The bass player in our band says he doesn't like rehearsing too much, saying that it kills the spontaneity of a performance and that he would far rather leave a few things to chance just to keep him on edge during a gig. Is it true that you can over-rehearse?

**A:** When someone asks me something like this all I can think about is what would happen if the Red Arrows had the same attitude towards rehearsing, preferring to 'leave some things to chance' during a display! But seriously, a lot of musicians I've talked to over the years have said that you simply can't be over-prepared for a performance, but you do have to be reasonable and reach some sort of realistic compromise, at the same time.

When you go and see a top pro band perform, it often looks like they're not even thinking about what they're playing and it's probably true to say that they're not. Worrying whether you'll remember the next chord sequence or if you'll handle the tricky piece in the next song are signs that there is still work to do in the rehearsal room, either individually (if it's one of you who keeps fouling up) or collectively if it's something you have to sequence as a unit.

I would imagine that a good yardstick to apply is that if your performance of any given song is consistently good every time you play it, then that piece has been properly rehearsed. If there are any elements of doubt or any regular 'train crashes' then there is still a lot of work to be done. Remember that it won't ever be 'all right on the night' if it still sounds like amateur hour in the rehearsal room!

**Q:** I've practised intensely over the past few years and managed to gain a considerable level of technical skill on the guitar, but at a recent jam session I was completely floored. I couldn't tell what was going on – and we were just trying to play a simple pop song. Where am I going wrong?

**A:** It sounds like you have been concentrating all your efforts on achieving an advanced technical level of playing and letting the other side of learning slip somewhat. You see, music has two sides: there's the pure nuts and bolts of learning the technique associated with any particular instrument – literally learning to operate the music machine in your hands.

Then there's the actual language of music itself, with an emphasis on ear training. To further demonstrate this important difference, I can obviously read music and I have immersed myself in theory books sufficiently so that I know the music landscape quite well – but I can't play flute or piano because I have zero technique on those particular instruments.

As you learn any instrument, these two sides must remain in perfect balance, or you run into the sort of embarrassing situation that you describe – either you wind up with insufficient technique to play the music you need to play, or you don't have the ear to lead you into the unknown with an appropriate and almost divine level of inspired intuition!

You need to return to the woodshed and concentrate on ear training and it wouldn't hurt to read some books on basic music theory, too.

If you are computer friendly, seek out some of the excellent ear training programmes that are available on the internet. This type of learning is invaluable as you can usually find time every day to spend a few minutes with your computer and, because it takes on the nature of a game, it can actually be fun at the same time.

Where books are concerned, you need to seek out those that have been written for the exam syllabus. In the UK, these are the Associated Board books I and II by Eric Taylor (readily available from most book stores). These will take you over the fundamental terminology which should fill in some of the blanks.

Finally, finding a teacher is a good idea in order to pace or coach you while you teach yourself. You would probably only need one lesson a month as this sort of learning cannot and must not be rushed otherwise it will be channelled into your short-term memory and not into the long-term where it needs to be. If you can find a teacher who is prepared to coach you through some ear training on this basis, all well and good. Ask the right questions during the initial phone call and all should be well as most good teachers are prepared to offer 'custom packages' to suit individual pupils.

**Q:** Our band recently got a new vocalist and he's really good, but the trouble is that a lot of the songs we've learned are out of his range – he's got a much higher voice than the last guy. The new singer says we can just change the keys around to suit his voice, but I haven't a clue where to start. He's a really good singer and we don't want to lose him. Any clues?

**A:** There are two methods you can use: the easy option is to buy a capo and move it up the fretboard to the desired key and the other involves a little more work...

Fist of all, using a capo may not sound too cool for an electric player, but it certainly didn't do Muddy Waters, Mark Knopfler or Albert Collins any harm! That way you can play all of the same chord shapes you played originally, just a bit higher up the neck.

If this isn't an option, you'll have to learn how to transpose the songs you know into the new singer's chosen keys. The quick and easy method is to write out two scales: the one belonging to the original key and the new one, like this. Let's say we want to transpose from C to G:

```
C   D   E   F   G   A   B   C
G   A   B   C   D   E   F♯  G
```

If the chords in the original key were C, F and G, you just check your diagram and find that C becomes G, F becomes C and G becomes D. So your new version of the song will contain the chords G, C and D. As I said, it's slightly more laborious and occasionally you'll find that the new key throws up some awkward chord changes, but it's a system that works.

**Q:** How do you get to transcribe chords from CDs? I just can't seem to hear what's going on most of the time and have to try to find a transcription from somewhere before I can play a song. Is there anything I can practise that will help?

**A:** Transcribing from CDs is something practically everyone can learn how to do – all it takes is some serious ear training. The more you are able to 'tune your ear' into music's funny little ways, the easier you'll find it to pick out chord arrangements and solos from recordings.

You might want to buy some software that slows down pieces from CDs but keeps the pitch the same, so that you can literally go through a song or solo note by note.

Personally, I use one called 'Transcribe!' which is available from www.seventhstring.com, and this particular programme comes with a chord analyser that will help you recognise the notes within chords while your ear develops.

**Q:** I am 40 years old and would love to attend the guitar weekends or summer schools I see advertised or even enquire about some of the guitar institutes, how do these places feel about us more mature students?

**A:** The courses that you mention welcome players of all ages and would certainly do you a great deal of good as you would be mixing with other players and this alone can prove invaluable.

Take a good look at the websites of institutions like the International Guitar Festival in Bath (www.igf.org.uk) and see if there is anything there that interests you.

**Q:** How do I get a really powerful rock guitar sound at low volumes? I've tried just about every tone setting on my Marshall practice amp, but they all sound a bit thin. What am I doing wrong?

**A:** I'd say that the simplest answer here is that you can't! If we're talking about low strung grunge rock, then that sound certainly depends on drop tuning and high volume as part of the overall sonic experience.

All we can do at lower volumes is to try and replicate the way a guitar responds under the fingers at high volume but not necessarily the way it sounds, as part of the overall sound picture is the speakers interacting with the cabinet and the valves working hard within the amp itself.

You might be better off checking out some headphone amplifiers – many of them have computer-based simulations built into them that compensate for low-volume practice and deliver the 'virtual' effect of a large amp being driven hard.

Your neighbours will love you for it, too!

**Q:** I recently attended my first band rehearsal and was a bit shocked to find that my sense of timing is awful. It wasn't that I was out of time with the drummer, I seemed to be out of time with everyone! Is there a way I can work on my rhythm so that it gets better? I really don't want to end up getting thrown out of the band.

**A:** This is quite a common syndrome when you first start playing with a band as everyone's sense of ensemble rhythm needs a certain amount of fine tuning.

In order to learn some rhythm discipline you need to start practising with either a metronome or a drum machine. Set a slow speed and begin by playing simple chord arrangements or scales along with the basic pulse, making sure that everything is in sync at all times. When you're absolutely sure that everything is in time, gradually increase the speed.

If you spend a few weeks working with a metronome, you'll soon find that your rhythm playing improves.

**Q:** I find it really hard to remember chord arrangements to songs I'm learning. A friend of mine and I bash around on a couple of acoustics and we've agreed to play at a barbeque in a few weeks but I don't know if I'll be able to remember anything without a crib sheet. As it is I have to write everything we play out and keep it where I can see it and it just doesn't look too professional. How do guys in bands remember stuff? It's not like we don't rehearse or anything, we're playing together two or three times a week.

**A:** It might be that relying on your 'crib sheets' is exactly where you're going wrong. As long as they are there, you don't actually need to remember the chord arrangements and so there's nothing to encourage you to commit them to memory. You need to begin the memorising process by abandoning your crib sheets and trying to remember the chord arrangements as best you can in the practice room. It's just like learning a poem or a speech – you'll remember so much and have to refer to your notes occasionally as a prompt. Be strict – no cheating; I'll bet that you do a lot better than you think. Gradually, your memory will get better and you'll need to refer to your crib sheets less and less – but the first step is to turn them over and trust your ability to process the material through all the right channels!

**Q:** Are there right and wrong ways to rehearse?

**A:** Definitely. One of the usual misconceptions about band rehearsals is that it's an opportunity merely to play together, rather than do any serious work. So a lot of time gets wasted running through the band's set, playing material you can already play in your sleep whilst no time at all is given over to new material or ironing out any problems that have cropped up on previous gigs.

Ideally, if you want to run through material it should be in the form of getting intros and endings right. Literally play the beginning, one verse and the end of each piece, just to make sure everyone is collectively on the ball. If anyone isn't sure what he should do at a certain point in a song, isn't sure if what he's playing really 'fits' or wants to experiment with something slightly different, then it should be a simple matter of asking the band to play through that section a couple of times. You might find that the average rehearsal comprises lots of little bits and pieces like this – and it's a constructive evening's work if it is. If you still want to wind the amps up and play, have a jam at the end of the rehearsal and see what happens.

# 10: GETTING GIGS

*If you have rehearsed to a good level of performance, the next thing to do is to go out and play – but first, you have to find some gigs...*

**Q:** How does a new band go about getting gigs?

**A:** Unless you live somewhere impossibly rural, it's quite likely that there's a few pubs in the area who have live music one or two days a week. What you need to do initially is to check out what kind of bands they put on from a stylistic viewpoint – the local paper is a good place to start – and then invest in a couple of nights out to go and see some performances. If you have recorded a demo – which is always a good idea in any case – see if you can find out from the bar staff who is responsible for booking the bands and ask if you can have a few words. Bear in mind that bar staff are busy people and so don't start with your life story – it's usually sufficient to introduce yourself, leave your demo and ask if it's OK to call back either by phone or in person in a week or so to discuss any possible bookings.

You will probably find that a lot of places are booked up quite far in advance, so you may well have the unexpected luxury of time to rehearse a bit more!

You might also find that some venues have 'quiet nights' where they put on new bands just to try them out. These can be on an 'expenses only' basis in many cases and so you won't receive a fee, but it will give you a chance to rehearse a bit in public and let the landlord see that you're a viable outfit to put on in his pub.

The relationship between band and landlord is always a strained one, in my experience, and I could tell you loads of horror stories connected with playing in pubs. The transaction is based on the fact that you want to play in public and get paid for doing so and the landlord wants to sell beer. Simple as that. If both boxes are ticked, you're on to a winner, but if you end up playing to an empty pub, no one goes home happy.

No matter how good your band is and how serious you are about playing 30-minute long Grateful Dead covers, if people don't come along to listen, you're flogging a dead horse!

**Q:** I'm a singer songwriter – how do I get a gig?

**A:** If you mean that it's just you, an acoustic guitar and a repertoire of your own material or tasteful covers, then probably the best place to start is to look around to see if anyone in the area holds 'open mike nights'. Basically, what happens here is that the venue will provide a PA and a couple of mikes and relies on local singers and instrumentalists to come along and play a few tunes. It's a bit like speed dating with music...

This is certainly an ideal way of trying out your material on a small crowd, before you think about taking things any further. It's good experience, too.

After that, it's really a similar strategy to the one I've outlined in the previous question; look for venues who put on music in your stylistic area, take along a demo, or even offer to come along at a quiet time and audition (something that's a lot easier when you're a soloist!).

It might involve a lot of phone calls and legwork, but once you begin to build a reputation, you'll perhaps find that people start seeking you out, rather than the other way around.

## Q: Do I need to join the Musicians' Union?

**A:** If you're thinking of performing at anywhere near professional levels, then it's probably a good idea to at least look into it, yes. I contacted the MU and they very kindly gave me permission to quote from their literature, regarding the benefits of membership...

'The Musicians' Union is an organisation respected around the world which represents over 30,000 musicians working in all sectors of the music business. As well as negotiating on behalf of musicians with all the major employers in the industry, the MU offers a range of services tailored for the self-employed by providing assistance for full- and part-time professional and student musicians of all ages.

Endeavouring to promote the rights and interests of its members, the MU strives to ensure technological advances are harnessed to promote more work opportunities for musicians. The Musicians' Union has specialist full-time officials available to immediately tackle the issues raised by musicians working in the live arena, the recording studio, or when writing and composing. Such issues can range from copyright protection to valuable contractual advice or from the recovery of unpaid fees to crucial work in health and safety.'

For further information, check out the MU website at www.musiciansunion.org.uk.

## Q: Who organises the publicity for a gig?

**A:** I'll refer you to the answer to a similar question on page 127 to get the promoter's angle on publicity for gigs – but I thought I'd deal with an alternative answer here, if you've arranged the gig yourself. Basically, if you haven't been booked through an agent or promoter, then it's quite likely that publicity is down to you. But in all cases, it's essential to communicate with someone at the venue to see exactly what the situation is regarding publicising acts appearing there. If in doubt, ask, in other words.

There's no such thing as having too much publicity for a gig and so it's probably a good idea to get in touch with any local gig guides – in your local paper, for instance – and check out the local radio stations to see if they give live music a mention at all.

In these days of desktop publishing, it's not hard to put together some flyers or even posters inexpensively and so if any of you have the necessary computer skills (or know someone who does) it's always worth running some off and seeing if local businesses (and the venue itself) will display them for you. Lastly, if you have a website, make sure it's updated regularly with news of upcoming gigs – and if you're really busy, it's always worth seeing if you can implement a mailing list so that you can keep your fanbase informed of your activities.

## Q: Do I need a contract to play at a pub?

**A:** Technically, no. A lot of pub gigs are strictly 'casual' and some landlords don't like the idea of 'having to sign something' just to let you play at their venue.

However, bear in mind that agreeing to turn up at a certain time on a certain date and play for a specified length of time is in itself a contract and it's up to you to ensure that each party is fully informed as to the needs of the other at all times. Ask how early you can arrive to set up, check if there's a 'curfew' (i.e. a time when you must stop playing so that the venue's relationship with neighbours, etc, remains on an even keel). If you anticipate everything that might turn into a misunderstanding well in advance and sort it out, everything should be fine.

*I get a lot of questions about the role of the promoter. In order to expore this area, I'll hand you over to Tim Orchard... Tim is a musician, songwriter, record collector and sometime music writer. He promotes live music for Purr Promotions and is one half of Purr Records with his colleague and good friend David Tinkham. Purr Promotions promote the music they want to hear in the hope that others will like it too. They were born on 13th January 2000.*

*Purr's current venue of choice is Invention in Bath. For more details on Purr Promotions or Purr Records visit www.purr.org.uk, www.myspace.com/purrlive & www.myspace.com/purrrecords*

## Q: What does a promoter do?

**A:** 'A promoter's job is to book a band, or a bill of musically compatible bands, to play at a specific venue on a specific date for an agreed fee. This can be for a one-off event, as part of a tour, or on a club night. The fee is either fixed and agreed in advance or an agreed percentage of the door takings after costs have been deducted.

If a promoter books a band through an agency, a contract is drawn up, the contents of which are signed up to by the band's management or representative and the promoter. The contract normally requests that the promoter provides, at least, a PA system, lights and refreshments.

The promoter also agrees to promote the event to ensure the venue has an attendant audience in keeping with its capacity and the artiste's audience potential. This usually involves the promoter writing a press release which they then email with print-ready publicity photos to local and national press. In addition to this, some promoters will provide CDs to local, national and student radio. Most, at least, will have a website and/or MySpace (ie www.myspace.com) with MP3s and downloadable publicity materials available. The promoter will also produce and distribute posters and flyers to advertise each individual event he/she promotes. Prior to the event, the promoter will normally contact the bands playing with arrival, sound check, stage times and directions. Some promoters will also provide information on places to stay.

Many promoters put the bands in touch with one another, too. If the bands playing have been in contact with one another prior to the event it usually makes for a smoother running show and an upbeat atmosphere, with equipment sharing and mutual appreciation oiling the wheels.

A good promoter will listen to the bands they book in advance, and do their best to put on a coherent and entertaining show.'

## Q: What does a promoter expect from a band?

**A:** 'A promoter expects a band to:

• promote the date and venue to their fanbase
• provide the promoter with publicity materials (biog/press/high-res photos/mp3s)
• communicate any specific sound, lighting and/or dietary requirements to the promoter prior to the night of the show
• not change musical direction between setting up the show and arriving at the venue
• in the case of some venues, avoid playing other shows in the same town too near to the date
• turn up at the requested time with the same line-up that has been publicised
• bring functional equipment
• respect the fact that other bands need to sound check as well
• entertain the audience, not outstaying their welcome (as in, observe their allotted stage time)

• not break anything that doesn't belong to them on or off stage
• mix with the other bands
• be agreeable towards the sound engineer and listen to his/her comments
• enter into the spirit of the occasion
• respect the venue's neighbours on their departure.'

**Q:** If I want a club to book my band, do I send them a demo?

**A:** 'Visit the promoter's website. If bands like your own regularly play for the promoter, by all means send him/her a demo. Alternatively, email the promoter a link to your website or MySpace. Initially, a promoter needs to hear your songs, read your press and see your photo(s). A promoter does not need a demo from a band that are the antithesis of his/her musical policy.'

**Q:** What can a band do to help promote a gig?

**A:** 'Bands should use all available means (websites / MySpace / word-of-mouth / publicity /mailouts) to communicate the shows they play to their fanbase (and beyond). Most live music events can benefit from being part of carefully constructed tours, promoting high-profile releases.

The symbiotic nature of the agent / band / promoter relationship necessitates a need for mutual understanding and good communication.'

# 11: PERFORMING LIVE

*The central core of many musicians' lives is the time they spend on stage performing. If they are not actually out there doing it, you can be sure that they are planning or preparing for it in some way. The top pros work with a kind of dedicated self-discipline that few 'outsiders' can understand. Social lives are often seriously disrupted or even completely put on hold in order that there be sufficient time for practice, rehearsal and performance – and this obviously can have an adverse effect on personal relationships and family life. But many will agree that live performance beats any artificial stimulant you can name and that all the dedication and self-denial is often well worth it.*

*It's obviously an area that generates a lot of questions from the novice, too...*

**Q:** **What sort of thing do I need to take with me on a gig (apart from a guitar and amp, of course!)**

**A:** To begin with, I'd suggest that you make yourself up a tool kit comprising everything you need to make 'roadside repairs' to gear on the night. Things like screwdrivers, allen keys, spare fuses (both mains fuses and the type that are used internally in amplifiers), a sharp knife, pliers – and so on. Then make sure that you are carrying spare strings, leads, batteries for effects units or your guitar tuner, etc – try to think ahead and see if you can deal with any upsets. You can't carry a spare for everything, but it's advisable to be as prepared as is practical.

Apart from the above, things like good, sturdy guitar stands are a must – I've heard of guitars getting broken on stage too many times because they were lent carelessly against an amplifier or drum riser and knocked over!

Then there are things you should keep with you in the car – a good, bright torch for helping with loading and unloading in badly lit pub car parks, for instance. Make sure your mobile phone is fully charged before you leave and that you have a contact number at the venue just in case you are held up. Remember that communication is everything. Also, you need a good, up to date

road atlas (unless you have Sat Nav, in which case you can skip this bit...) because some places are extraordinarily hard to find – especially in the dark.

**Q:** **What sort of 'pre-gig etiquette' is it best to adopt?**

**A:** Keep in touch with the promoter or your contact at the venue and make sure everyone knows exactly what's happening. Negotiate a time when you can load in the gear so that you have time to sound check before the doors open to the public (this can be a luxury at a pub gig, but possible in a lot of clubs and other similar venues). Turn up on time, be polite, do the job to the best of your ability and go home. It really ought to be as simple as that.

**Q:** **What sort of things can go wrong on a gig?**

**A:** The simple answer is 'everything'. Quite often it's a case of being under-prepared or the flow of communication between venue and band not being as good as it needs to be. I'll give you a couple of examples...

I did a gig once at a country house. When the band arrived – me, a pianist and bass player – we asked where we should set up and were told that there was a marquee in the (sizeable) garden. When we checked, though, we found that the marquee was candle-lit – very romantic, but we needed power and none had been run out there. So we had to compromise and set up indoors, which was far from ideal and could have been sorted in advance if only people had talked to each other sooner.

On another occasion, we turned up to play at a pub in Felixstowe for a summer barbecue. This time, I was with a jazz fusion band that had guitar, bass, keyboards, drums, trumpet – and a full PA. Once again, we asked where we should set up and the bar staff directed us to a section of the pub they had cleared ready for our arrival.

But there were no power sockets at all. So we mentioned this to the landlord and he told us he'd unplug the juke box when we were ready to start playing... And one power point for a whole band isn't a particularly good (or safe) idea.

Both of the above could have been sorted earlier, as I say, by simple communication prior to the gig, but life in a band is a learning curve, as they say...

Other things that can go wrong would range from power cuts, equipment failure or damage – you name it. As I've said earlier, the only talisman that works is to carry enough spares as you can and try to out-think the gremlins that make things go wrong in the first place.

**Q:** Are there any major differences from doing a gig at your local and a pro gig in a hall?

**A:** Not as many as you might think, no – certainly not from a musical point of view as I'm assuming that your set would be pretty much the same for both types of venue. You'll probably have the luxury of a larger stage and so there's more room to spread out the gear and generally move around a bit while you're playing, which is nice. I've played in venues where I didn't dare move in case I took the bass player's eye out with my guitar's headstock!

You will need to check things like PA because if you carry your own and it's powerful enough for a pub gig, it might sound a little lost in a large hall. You might also have to think about miking instruments up – or even consider asking the venue or promoter whether they will help out with the hire of a larger system that comes with an engineer and crew.

You will certainly need monitors, too – a lot of bands try to get by without monitoring in smaller pub type venues (although this is getting increasingly rare as house PA systems have improved enormously in recent times and portable rigs have become a lot more affordable, too) but they are essential for larger gigs.

It often comes as quite a shock to people to realise that they can't hear anything on a large stage except possibly their own amp (and that is not guaranteed, either). If the bass player has set up on the other side of the stage you won't hear a note he plays, under normal circumstances.

Apart from that, you might want to ask about lights – most halls have some kind of stage lighting in place, but the chances are it won't be very rock'n'roll. If the venue is used to putting on bands, then this will probably have been sorted out beforehand, but it's desperately important to check.

This is why professional bands often have contracts which are many pages thick; everything from the width, height and depth of the stage to the number of dressing rooms available will have been noted and accounted for.

Ask about loading, too. Some venues have stages that have been designed with a marvellous amount of easy access for loading and unloading (I played a venue once where the whole of the back of the stage opened up to give access to the car park at truck height – fantastic!). But there are still some venues where the only way to get your gear on stage is to haul it up two separate spiral staircases!

There used to be a book available which had listings of most of the gig venues and included details like access, power supply, etc, but I haven't seen one in a while, which is unfortunate because it was a great idea and very useful, too.

Finally, there's attitude to consider; if you have it in mind that the job's the same irrespective of the size of venue or amount of people who make up the audience (whom you won't be able to see because the lights will be in your eyes) then you'll be able to keep on an even keel.

**Q:** Is there some sort of rule that determines when it's right to use the bridge or neck pickup? I thought jazz players use the neck pickup and rock players use the bridge, but my Les Paul says 'rhythm' and 'lead' on the selector switch, indicating that we're meant to use the neck for rhythm playing.

**A:** You should know by now that there are no rules in rock and roll! Seriously, the choice of pickup is very individual and very much integral to the style of the player.

Many players make full use of all selections available, others will stick with one and leave it pretty much alone. Eric Clapton will use the neck pickup on his Strat as a default, playing both rhythm and lead and will occasionally switch to the middle pickup for a thinner sound (you can see him do this on the Cream Albert Hall video).

Knopfler will stick with one of the so called 'out of phase' Strat pickup selections for the most part and it has become part of his overall signature sound.

Don't worry about what appears to be right – this pickup for lead, this for rhythm – use your ears and go with the sound that seems right to you.

**Q:** I went to an open mic session at a local club the other night, fully intending to sing a couple of songs I've been learning, but when I was called up I just couldn't do it. I was just frozen to the floor and getting up on stage would have been like jumping off a cliff! I want to get into a little bit of casual performing, but if I'm going to have to go through this every time I won't be able to – there must be a way around it; can you help?

**A:** What you experienced was stage fright – something that has been around since people started performing in front of each other aeons ago. Even the very best performers get nervous before walking on stage, but have learned to control it and re-route the nervous energy so that it becomes positive rather than negative.

A great many people have found the book *The Inner Game Of Music* by Barry Green and Timothy Gallway immensely helpful in this respect. Try tracking down a copy and reading it – I'm sure it will help!

**Q:** My band have been offered a PA system at a very reasonable price, owing to another band splitting up and selling off all its co-operatively owned equipment. They've given us two prices, one for the PA and one for the monitors, which is obviously quite a bit extra. My question is, do we need monitors or can we get by with just the basic PA cabs and mixer amp? The band is two guitarists (one of us sings) a bass player (providing harmony vocals) and drummer.

**A:** To be honest, it's worth spending the extra money and buying the monitors. Even fairly modest PA systems that are used exclusively for vocals benefit from having monitors because, as I'm sure you're aware, being onstage with a rock band is a noisy experience and if the singers can hear themselves – and the rest of the band can hear them, too – it's more likely that everyone will play together better and the singers will be in tune. If you've never played through a PA with monitors before, you'll wonder how you managed once you've done so.

I once played a gig in a 1,500 seater auditorium with a large PA system and no monitors and it was like trying to play in a vacuum as no one on stage could hear anything other than their own instrument. Not a situation I'd recommend under any circumstances!

**Q:** It's my first gig with a new band and I want to do things right – what advice can you give me?

**A:** Basically, I'd say that if it's the first gig with a new band, you need to turn up on time, having learned all your parts well, don't make a fuss or throw any tantrums, do the job as professionally as you can, get along with people in general and go home.

The fact is that there's not really anything like the 'perfect playing experience' and so you can expect a few glitches, either in terms of the material not going quite right, or some point regarding the actual organisation of the event having got a little skewed or misunderstood between band and venue management.

I've always found it wise to accept a compromise at the time and find out how to avoid the same situation cropping up in the future is the best line to take. It's a learning curve – which is fine, as long as you actually learn from it!

**Q:** How long do we have to play for?

**A:** It varies. The 'standard' is probably two 45–60 minute long sets, but it's always advisable not to take this for granted and check with the venue well in advance, preferably at the time the gig is booked. You may need to adjust your fee if you are expected to play after midnight or do three sets instead of two.

**Q:** Is it true we can claim overtime from a venue if we're asked to play longer than originally agreed?

**A:** Ideally, yes – as long as it's made clear from the start that any extra work on the part of the band is subject to the fee being re-negotiated on the night. This is the value of having some sort of contract between you and the venue, as both parties know the requirements of the other in advance.

**Q:** What happens if a venue refuses to pay the band?

**A:** If communication has broken down with the venue's management in this respect, you need to seek legal advice immediately. If you were working with a contract, then you would have to be prepared to prove that you either fulfilled or were at least in a position to fulfil your side of it on the night. If you are a member of the Musicians' Union, they can help you, but if not, you'll need to seek reimbursement via the small claims procedure in the courts, if things can't be sorted out otherwise.

To be honest, this sort of thing hardly ever happens – so don't go out there expecting the worst. Once again, if a good relationship between band/promoter and venue has been struck in the first place, petty grievances on behalf of any of the parties involved can usually be sorted out amicably without the need to resort to legal action.

**Q:** What sort of preparations do I need to make guitar-wise before a gig?

**A:** If you gig regularly then you'll be aware how often you need to change strings and you'll be conscious of the state your equipment is in, too. If you're just setting out or only gig occasionally then it's as well to put on a new set of strings, give your guitar the once over to make sure there's nothing obvious that needs attention, change the batteries in effect units and your tuner – and make sure that your amp is working and generally crackle free.

As long as you take my advice about carrying as many spares as is practicable, you should be OK.

**Q:** What sort of thing can I ask for on a rider?

**A:** To begin with, I'd invite you to read Slim's (from The Hamsters) comments on riders on page 111. Don't be tempted to overdo it just to satisfy your ego – if you need bottled water on stage, or clean towels, etc then you could always consider carrying them yourself.

The unreasonable – and a lot of the time comical – requests for backstage luxuries are the province of the millionaire status bands. Outrageous requirements at a provincial level aren't likely to endear you to the venue's management or promoter.

The illusion that contract riders are free 'extras' isn't true either, as someone, somewhere has to pay for the items you request – and it's probably you, at the end of the day!

**Q:** Why do some guitarists put their amps on beer crates at a gig?

**A:** Most of the time it's purely to get them off the floor and bring them up to a height whereby they a) look cool and b) you can hear them/make adjustments to levels, etc without bending down.

Occasionally you'll see little 'amp risers' in touring bands which are designed to minimise the variable acoustic effects that different stages sometimes impose.

I know of one guitarist who regularly tours with a major name band who had some hollow wooden plinths specially made for his amps because they didn't sound right if the stage was made from either metal or concrete and his amps were set up directly on top. The resonance of the wood gives him a more consistent sound from night to night.

**Q:** What happens if I break a string mid-song?

**A:** Let's face it; everyone breaks strings and they rarely do so at a convenient moment. If you've put a fresh set on before the gig, it's unlikely you'll get a breakage (although this is by no means guaranteed) but if it happens and you don't have a spare guitar nearby, you'll have to make do until you can change it. Sometimes you'll find there's someone you know in the audience who can offer 'roadside assistance'. I once played a gig where the bass player and keyboard player had managed to forget to bring the PA power amp with them (each thought the other had packed it) and, if it wasn't for the fact that one of my students happened to be in the audience that night and he was able to run home and fetch his band's power amp for us to use we'd have suddenly become an instrumental unit...

Oh, and I once saw Jimmy Page break a string during a Led Zeppelin gig at Wembley Arena – he didn't miss a note!

**Q:** It's really difficult to set a sound up on my amp when I play live. If I think I'm sounding really bad, someone invariably comes up afterwards and says what a great sound I had – what do I do?

**A:** Experience is really the best teacher here, as this is a well-known phenomenon. If you're playing at gig volumes – and particularly if you are using a combo – it's likely that the full timbre of your amp will only become apparent about 20 feet away as it takes this distance for the sound to spread out into the room (a little like firing a shotgun). During your sound check, get someone to stand a few feet into the audience while you adjust the pre amp controls on your amp. Or alternatively, pack a long lead so that you can walk a few feet away and check out what you sound like in the room while you set up your sound. It means a lot of extra walking about, but hey, art is pain, right?

Remember that rooms absorb certain frequencies and you might have to over-compensate for this at source. Also, empty rooms sound different to those full of sweaty, beer-swilling bodies and so you may well end up tweaking your amp settings slightly once the performance starts.

The end result might be that you think you're sounding thin and trebly whilst the audience is celebrating your sonic loveliness from a safe distance.

This doesn't apply when you're miking your amp up through a PA, of course. Here, a live sound engineer will often request you to get a good sound from your amp close-to and then mic it accordingly.

## Q: Do we need to mic up the amps on the average pub gig?

A: It's true to say that more and more bands are miking instruments up these days, because of the extra flexibility and control it gives them over the band's overall sound and balance.

It can mean quieter on-stage volume levels, too, as the backline amps don't need to project to the extremities of the venue; but if you don't own a PA and have to resort to hiring, it can be an expensive business and smaller gig fees aren't likely to make it too cost effective unless you're a band that gigs regularly.

Some venues have quite good house PA systems now and so it can sometimes be a case of following their lead as to whether it's necessary or not, seeing as they know the acoustics at the venue better than you do yourself.

It is possible to put on a very good performance without going to the lengths of miking everything in smaller venues – let's face it, some of the biggest bands in the world did this kind of gig for years back at the dawn of rock'n'roll where all the power resided in the backline – and so I wouldn't fret about it too much.

## Q: I plugged my acoustic guitar into my amp and it immediately fed back horribly – what can I do?

A: Well, you could try not plugging your acoustic into your amp! If you use a PA, you can route your acoustic's signal through that via a direct box (or DI box as they're sometimes called) which is essentially an interface between an instrument and the PA amplifier that keeps signal levels on track.

Failing this, you should look to invest in a special acoustic guitar amplifier – there are plenty on the market and a few minutes on the internet will reveal most of the principal manufacturers.

Electric guitar amplification is very different from the specialist type that deals with acoustic guitars as we are talking about a different level and type of signal. Add this to the fact that the EQ on an acoustic guitar amp will have to be calibrated to accommodate the frequency range and characteristics of the instrument, and you can begin to see why your electric guitar amp had a fit when you tried to plug your acoustic into it.

I'm not saying that you won't experience feedback problems with an acoustic amp (or even a PA) but at least all your electrical components will be reading from the same script, so to speak.

## Q: Is it necessary to soundcheck for a pub gig?

A: Yes, I think it is. But let's not forget that there is a huge difference between unnecessary widdling or cacophonous ensemble instrument pounding and a disciplined run through to make sure everything is sounding OK and working up to spec. Ideally, everyone should get a 'sound' together from their gear one at a time and then the whole band play through a few bars of something just to get the balance right. Make any adjustments as necessary and walk away. Stick to these rules and publicans and club owners will applaud your professionalism!

*At some larger gigs or festivals, it's likely that you will be working with a stage manager. In order to answer the next series of questions on the duties of such an individual, I called upon Alex Pym, an excellent stage manager with whom I've often worked in the past. Alex graduated from RADA in 1986 with a diploma in stage management, worked in theatre for several years including New End Theatre (stage manager) and the National Theatre, Southbank (on the lighting crew).*

*He also organised concerts and ran festival stages for the Musician's Network 1991–95. Alex has played guitar since the age of 14 and completed major tours, playing venues such as Brixton Academy and the Astoria. He's also played festivals (including Glastonbury and Glade) and appeared on BBC TV's Top of The Pops.*

*He currently plays in Dream Machine and ZubZub (both featuring ex-members of Ozric Tentacles – CDs and DVDs completed), teaches guitar (since 1990) and is a member of The Registry of Guitar Tutors (RGT).*

*He has been stage manager for the International Guitar Festival in Bath since 2003.*

**Q:** What does a stage manager do?

**A:** 'The stage manager is responsible for running the show/concert. He or she has to make sure that the artists are happy, that the show starts and ends on time and basically oversees all departments (lighting/sound/crew) – making sure that everything runs smoothly.

A good stage manager (SM) should be like a good football referee – practically invisible.

The main trick is to anticipate everything that could go wrong and prevent it from happening, and basically it's just common sense. I was trained in stage management at RADA – which helps – but a music event is very different to stage managing a theatre show, which will have had weeks of rehearsals and at least three full technical rehearsals.

In the world of live music only massive shows like a Pink Floyd world tour would you have everything as organised.

Your average gig/concert is usually a trip into the unknown and, in short, anything can happen and the chances of things going wrong are obviously increased.

The SM has to co-ordinate all the various departments at a gig, most of whom will not have met before. The artist may have specific lighting requirements and it's your job to relay this information to the correct personnel at the venue.

Ideally, you want everyone to discuss the forthcoming concert in detail, but very often there simply isn't the time because people always seem to be running late. Sometimes you don't even get a chance to do a soundcheck!

Ideally, a spec sheet should have been sent in advance along with the rider (drinks and food requirements) and any specific lighting, sound or stage requests (such as a drum riser) that are required on the night. However, the spec sheet always seems to be out of date; I've spent hours chasing around for lists of stage requirements, arranging items from obscure percussion instruments to a piano stool, only to be told, 'Er, we don't need any of that...' by the band when they show up for the gig.

The problem is that these spec sheets are sent out by the agents and only infrequently updated, so a phone call to the artist or tour manager to check these requirements in advance can save hours of messing about.'

**Q:** What is the most crucial time for you at a gig?

**A:** 'The most important time for the stage manager is half an hour before the show begins. The SM gives the all clear for the front of house staff to open the doors to the public and then they will have to put out the towels, water and other requirements from the artists' rider onstage. I check that all the amps are turned on, effects pedals plugged in, etc and keep the artists and technical crew informed of the time, giving ten, five and two minute calls to alert everyone to the general countdown before show time. Once I get clearance from front of house, I will collect the artists from their dressing rooms and take them to the stage. I'll then tell the lighting and sound engineer that we're ready to go, the houselights dim and the band takes the stage...'

**Q:** What if there is a support act?

**A:** 'If there are support acts they will have set up in front of the headline act's equipment. The headline act will have sound checked first, leaving the support act to set up and soundcheck after them. The support act will not rearrange the headliner's equipment in any way (except in very unusual circumstances, like a chronic shortage of stage space or if they're sharing a drum kit). Then, during the interval, the stage manager will supervise and help 'striking' (removing) the support act's equipment. The SM will then give a five and two minute call to the headline artist and repeat the start of show sequence as above.'

**Q:** Is it true that a stage manager is employed by the venue as opposed to the band?

**A:** 'The stage manager should not be confused with the tour manager. The SM is nearly always employed by the venue or promoter and is responsible for the entire show. A tour manager is specifically in charge of the band and touring crew and so only on huge tours will the tour manager oversee everything. In that situation they would have an SM working under them to run the show and rehearsals.'

**Q:** What about festivals or outdoor gigs?

**A:** 'Running a festival stage with multiple band line-ups is perhaps the most stressful thing you can do as a stage manager. Time is your enemy: for example, you start at say 1 pm and you absolutely must be finished by midnight. If you start losing ten minutes here and five minutes there, by the time you get to your headline act there will be no time left. People will not be happy if they only get to see a 20-minute set by their favourite act – the one they've paid all the money for.

You have to allow for realistic changeover times between acts. All you need is one selfish artist to ignore you and hog the stage past their allotted time slot and you're in big trouble. A word of advice to anyone thinking of doing this... don't! You will seriously piss everybody off, especially the bands coming on after you – and the promoter, too. Promoters and concert organisers all know each other, word gets round and you will start losing gigs.'

**Q:** What's the difference between a stage manager and a roadie?

**A:** ''Roadies' are usually employed by the artist or tour manager to carry all the equipment in and out of the venue. They tour with the act on the road, hence the name. The 'roadies' are responsible for setting up the stage and putting all the amps, drum kits etc. in the right place. The term 'roadies' can also include the guitar and drum technicians, although some of them are so highly thought of that you would never refer to them as such. A top guitar tech with a major artist will be an expert in setting up, servicing and in all probability playing the guitar. Very often they will know far more about guitars than the artists themselves! If a venue supplies people to unload and set up equipment they would be referred to as stage or 'local' crew.'

**Q:** Has playing in a band yourself helped prepare you for a stage manager's duties?

**A:** 'Dealing with musicians and their problems requires a specific field of knowledge and I find that having played in bands for the past 25 years myself is a huge benefit to me at a gig. I know how to do a fast string change under pressure, because I've had to do it myself in front of an audience. I also know that the band won't listen to me when I tell them that they have to be finished by 10.30pm or the promoter will be fined by the local council for running over time. I know because I've been there myself. When you're on stage, time becomes an abstract concept where five minutes can seem like 30 seconds. So there's no use in me waiting until 10.25 pm and then telling them they've only got five minutes left. I've got to tell them closer to 10 pm, especially if they're going to do an encore.'

**Q:** Is there any sort of 'etiquette' to be observed at a performance?

**A:** 'Arrive on time! If you are late, keep the venue informed as to what's happening. This way the tech crew can eat, something they probably won't have time to do later, rather than just stand around waiting for you.

Stick to the stage times that you're given. Overrunning your time slot by more than a few minutes won't do you any favours. After all it's best to leave the audience wanting more, not less. Don't ask the SM to make you tea or coffee when they're busy, like 15 minutes before the show starts. It's an insult to their profession! They'll be happy to do it, if they have time, which is rare. Otherwise do it yourself...'

**Q:** Is it an enjoyable job?

**A:** 'Put it this way; over the years I've had the pleasure of working backstage with artists such as John Scofield, B. B. King, The Edge, Martin Taylor, Scott Henderson and Mick Taylor... to name a few. As a player and lover of guitar myself it has been awesome to work with these people. It has given me an insight that I would never have had otherwise.'

*Another professional you're likely to meet at larger gigs is the sound engineer. In order to illustrate exactly what his job entails – and how to carry out the consummate sound check – I'll hand you over to my colleague from the International Guitar Festival, Stuart McLean.*

*Stuart is a sound engineer who works in London and around the UK. He's played in, recorded with and led a number of bands in his native Canada and the UK. At one point, for a laugh, he took over doing sound for a night at a club in Canada and before he knew it was offered the job of house engineer. He then went on to get another house engineer job and soon found that about half his time was taken up by doing sound for bands.*

*Realising his musical dreams were being neglected, he fled to England where he completed a degree in music, majoring in composition, from the Liverpool Institute for Performing Arts (LIPA). He graduated with a first and had the honour of being the first student in the history of the Institute foolish enough to accept a commission to write music for its graduation ceremony.*

*Of course, in the real world, all this meant next to nothing, so to pay his exorbitant London rent he started doing sound again and now finds his time split between live concerts and events, producing albums for bands, and scoring short films in his home studio.*
*He's done sound in too many venues to list without boring people to death, but some of the highlights are the Cavern Club in Liverpool, the Sage in Gateshead, the Union Chapel in Islington and the Brixton Telegraph.*

*Stuart has also done sound at a number of outdoor festivals and, for the past four years has been the technical co-ordinator for the International Guitar Foundation.*

**Q:** **What are a live sound engineer's duties at a gig?**

**A:** 'Sound engineers have a variety of duties at a gig depending upon the size of the venue, but it all boils down to making the band sound as good as possible out front and on stage using whatever resources are available.'

**Q:** **What does a sound engineer want from a band at a soundcheck?**

**A:** 'The engineer wants to start off hearing each individual sound coming from the stage, be it a guitar amp, acoustic guitar DI, vocal microphone, or individual drum. The engineer also wants to hear the band play together so he can get a balance of instruments and vocals. For example, if you only have a couple of songs which have backing vocals, make sure you play through one of them during the sound check so that the engineer can get a balance of all the sounds he's likely to encounter during the gig.

Most importantly, the engineer wants to hear the instruments played in the way they will be played during the performance. If you play with massive distortion all night, then don't sound check on a wimpy clean sound. If you use both, let the engineer know and play a sample of your loudest and quietest sounds in the soundcheck. Playing your loudest is most important though, since you can cause some nasty sounding distortion through a system during your gig if you haven't played your loudest sound for the engineer in the soundcheck. Similarly, if you scream your vocals straight into the mic during the gig, don't spend your sound check whispering, 'Check… one… two…' from two feet away. Most vocal mics sound very different at a distance of half an inch than they do from two inches away and the volume of your voice makes a huge difference to the volume that comes out of the PA.'

**Q:** How can a band or musician best co-operate with a sound engineer?

**A:** 'The best thing musicians can do to co-operate with their engineer is simply listen to their advice when setting up for a gig. Unless you've already alienated your engineer by asking him or her to load in your gear while you take a fag break, the engineer is on your side and wants to make sure you sound great for the gig. If the engineer asks you to do something completely insane like turning your amp volume down, it's not because he wants to make sure no one hears your guitar solos.

Guitarists need to be aware that guitar amp speakers produce sound – particularly in the higher frequency ranges – that travels in a very straight line. Your amp might sound fine from where you're standing on stage, but ten feet out into the audience there could be a point where the treble is absolutely obnoxious. If your guitar amp sounds too loud where the engineer is standing, he won't put you through the PA, which means that a substantial part of the audience won't get the full effect of that amazing tapping solo in the third number.

One other thing to think about is that the speaker(s) in your guitar amp are probably worth £20, whereas the speakers in the PA system may be worth more than ten times that. What would you rather the audience heard your sound through? If the engineer asks you to turn down your amp below the point where you can comfortably hear it, ask him to put some of it back through the stage monitors.

Bass players should remember that some low frequencies their amps produce can't be heard properly until someone is more than ten feet away from the amplifier. If the sound engineer asks you to remove some low frequencies from your amp, he's not trying to destroy your tone – he's trying to make the whole band sound better.

Another important point to mention is that you should never play through your amp (or hit the drums) while the sound engineer is miking them up. I've never understood why many guitarists feel it's necessary to blast a power chord straight into the ears of the guy who is in charge of making a band sound good, at the point when he is closer to a guitar amp than any health and safety regulation should permit. Besides being rather insulting, you can (temporarily at least) damage the hearing of the guy who needs to hear better than anyone else in the room. (This sort of thing has happened to me so many times that I now wear earplugs when miking up.)'

**Q:** What's the difference between a 'sound check' and a 'line check'?

**A:** 'A sound check is generally a full, instrument-by-instrument test of the sound through the PA, during which time levels, E.Q., dynamics and effects are set up. A line check is a much quicker affair, usually done by the engineer alone and is more a check to see that everything on stage that needs to be is actually 'on line'.

All live sound mixing desks of professional quality include a 'PFL' (Pre Fader Level) or 'solo' button on each channel which will allow the engineer to listen to individual mics or line inputs like keyboards and DI'd acoustic guitars through a pair of headphones to make sure sound is coming through them. This can be done without any sound going through the speakers (this is especially useful at festivals where you're not supposed to interrupt a DJ set).'

**Q:** What sort of power do I need in a PA?

**A:** 'One of the most important things to remember when looking at buying or renting a PA is that in order to hear vocals clearly through it you'll need about ten times more wattage in your PA then you have in your guitar amp – particularly if it's a valve amp. If you need a 100 watt stack to hear your guitar when you're standing next to your muscle-bound, feral drummer, then you'll need at least 1000 watts of PA (that's at least

139

500 watts per side) pointing out from the front of the stage before the audience will be able to discern your deep, sensitive lyrics.

The good news is that most reasonable size clubs will have PAs of at least this size (and most small pubs will turn your kit off at the mains if you play this loud) so a good investment for many new bands is a small PA with about 400 watts (200 per side) or even a couple of powered wedge monitors. There are a huge variety of these types of system available in music stores or through newspaper ads.'

**Q:** Why are there sometimes separate sound engineers for the front of house and monitors?

**A:** 'At large gigs, such as theatres, concert halls and outdoor festivals, there is usually enough in the budget to have a separate mixer and engineer for front-of-house and stage monitor sound. This means that one engineer can focus entirely on the sound the audience hears while another engineer makes sure that everyone on stage gets the sound they want.

The monitor desk is usually on the side of stage, meaning that the band can talk to the engineer without speaking through the PA, using crude sign language, or writing things on the backs of their guitars (I'm sure I've seen a bass with 'less vox in mon' stencilled on the back!).

At festivals, the monitor engineer will place the mics on stage, since the front-of-house desk is often separated from the stage by heaving masses of fans and the front-of-house engineer is usually busy doing line checks, setting up the mix, fine tuning compressors or drinking coffee. Therefore it's a good idea to give a stage plot to both the monitor engineer and the front-of-house engineer.

Whether or not your monitors are controlled from the side of the stage or out front, make sure you let the appropriate sound engineer know if you need to hear more of a particular instrument or vocalist in your monitor. It's very frustrating when someone comes up to me after a gig is over and tells me they couldn't hear themselves the whole time, when, if they'd just let me know at any point during the gig I could have fixed it for them. Sound engineers, contrary to the way they often strut about, are not omnipotent and need to be told what things sound like up on stage. I personally don't think there's anything wrong with asking for more vocal in the monitor between songs (and it's definitely more professional than waving your arms and making obscene looking gestures to describe the lack of kick drum sound in your mix).

Within reason, keep pestering the engineer until you're happy with your sound on stage. (Note: turning your amp down might facilitate this process.)

It's also important to realise that there's a limit to how loud a microphone can be turned up in your monitors before it produces horrible, squealing feedback. If this happens, make sure the engineer is aware of it (although he or she probably heard it when you did). Some people seem to think it helps the engineer if they whistle the pitch of the feedback after it has stopped or show how clever they are by guessing the frequency the feedback was at, but personally, I find both of these 'tricks' unnecessary, and rather annoying.

**Coda:** one other little story which some people might find helpful:

I remember one gig when I was a house engineer where a guitarist turned up to a club an hour before soundcheck. While I was still getting the PA gear out, he set up his amp and pedals and started practising and noodling at a fairly loud volume. Just as the rest of the band had arrived, the manager of the club told me we would have to stop soundchecking, as patrons dining at the club were complaining about the noise. I told him that we hadn't even begun, to which he replied, 'Then what was all that noise about?'.

Because this guitarist had been playing unnecessary loudly for half an hour I was stuck in a very awkward situation – between the club manager and the band – and in the end the band wasn't able to get a proper soundcheck before the gig.'

# 12: THE RECORDING STUDIO

*There comes a time in every performer's life when he or she thinks it's time to put something down on CD for posterity. It might be a demo in order to get some live work, or it could be a self-financed first CD that they intend to sell at gigs. The common denominator here is the recording studio...*

**Q:** How do I find the right studio?

**A:** First of all, you need to work out exactly what your requirements are. If you're a singer-songwriter or essentially some kind of one-man or one-woman band, you'll only need a small studio in terms of physical size. If you're a band and want to lay down tracks by playing together, then you'll need to look for a studio that can accommodate this.

Next, ask around – local music shops, local bands in the area, etc, and see if anyone in particular comes with a high recommendation. This is quite likely as the smaller studios depend on a lot of their business from bands seeking to make either demos or CDs and so the good ones will probably have a local reputation.

Then it's down to making some calls and telling the studio representative exactly what you need in terms of time (and don't under-estimate here – just because some of rock'n'roll's iconic recordings have been made in a couple of days, doesn't mean you'll be able to follow suit!). It wouldn't be unreasonable to ask if you can visit the studio and meet people prior to making a decision regarding booking, either. This way you can make sure everything looks 'right' before making a commitment.

**Q:** What do I need to take with me into a studio?

**A:** Mainly, the equipment you are going to use during the recording, plus spare strings, tuner, leads and so on. It's wise to check what sort of facilities the studio has on offer well in advance – and, if possible, have a chat with the engineer beforehand as he might have some suggestions, too, based on what he knows will sound good in his studio.

Remember that something that sounds good in a live performance might not work in a studio for various reasons. I was told that my amp was unacceptably noisy in one, for instance, and ended up using one they had there which was smaller (physically) and less powerful, but quieter in performance and ultimately better sounding.

Keep an open mind and be ready to be guided by the studio engineer as he probably knows the best way to capture your sound and material.

**Q:** Is a producer really necessary?

**A:** Not for a demo – or even a DIY CD, I would say. The role of the producer is really someone who can act as an arbiter and overseer for the band, as well as taking care of the business end in many cases. He also acts as another set of (unbiased) ears behind the mixing desk and someone who can offer an opinion as to the quality of the material being produced.

Having said that, though, I was surprised when I interviewed the guitarist from a band that has become a household name and he told me that a producer was necessary for them from the point of view that he acted as a kind of 'headmaster' to the band, ensuring that they showed up on time, the instruments were in tune, lyrics were finished and everyone began and ended playing at the same time!

## Q: What's 'red light fever'?

**A:** This is a well-known syndrome in the studio where someone who knows what they are about to play really, really well, but always manages to fowl it up when it's time to record it. It's something we all do – practise a piece to perfection and then mess it up when it counts. It's usually all to do with nerves and the knowledge that what you're about to play is 'for posterity' and will be heard (hopefully) by many people. So you tense up and start making stupid mistakes...

The important thing here is that this is something everybody does and knows about and so it should be treated with intelligent disregard in the studio. If something isn't happening, don't begin to fret about it because that only makes matters worse. Adopt the attitude 'tomorrow's another day' and come back to it later on, giving the time over to something a little more mundane instead.

## Q: I've recorded some of my own material in a studio and people I've played it to think it's good enough to have it made into a CD. How do I go about this?

**A:** I'm assuming that your material has been mixed and that it is effectively 'ready to go', so the next stage is to have it mastered, ready for the duplication process (mastering is explained below). You have to decide how many copies of your CD you want to have made – and this all depends on how you're going to sell it. If you are intending to play live and sell your CDs at gigs or over the internet, you might want to think about getting around 1,000 pressed up, initially. If this proves not to be enough, you can always go back and have more pressed later as the pressing plant will keep a master copy. You'll need to make contact with a company who presses CDs – a quick search on the net will

reveal a few. Then ring around, or email them, try to get prices from them and make sure that the package you receive a quote on includes everything – printing the covers, booklets and so on. You're likely to be asked a lot of questions as there are always a lot of options available to you. If in doubt, ask the guy giving you the quote as some of the terminology in use can be confusing. It's a good idea to go into a record store and have a look at how CDs are packaged and the variations in terms of booklet size, etc, before making your call. It always pays to be informed, after all.

You'll have to apply for an MCPS licence to print, too – contact MCPS via their website at www.mcps-prs-alliance.co.uk. A CD pressing plant requires this licence before they can print up your CDs as it shows that any mechanical copyright due has been paid. You need to apply for the licence even if the CD contains only your own material, too. The form you need is downloadable at the website, but you will probably need to speak to someone at MCPS to guide you through it – they're usually very helpful – and the form is a lot easier to complete than it may seem initially. You will be asked what price you are going to be selling your CDs for as this forms the basis for the calculation as to what royalties are due from you (in the case of a CD with cover versions of other songwriters' material on).

You'll also be allowed a certain number of 'promotional' CDs for sending to newspapers, magazines and radio stations – and this is important because it effectively gives you a discount on the amount of royalties you have to pay. The maximum, at time of writing, is 250 promotional copies – and these have to be clearly marked 'Promotional copy – not for resale' in order to comply. Your pressing plant can sticker 250 copies for you at source, but it works out cheaper to get some stickers printed at a local printer and stick them on yourself.

While you're in touch with MCPS, you might want to find out about PRS, too – once again, speak to someone if you can't make sense of the website. In both cases, these organisations make sure that you are paid a royalty if your music is performed either live or played on the radio. This is important as, believe me, it's via songwriting royalties that musicians become rich!

If however, you're thinking more along the lines of distributing your CD amongst friends and family and have no intention to put it 'on sale' anywhere, then you need to look for a pressing plant that does small runs of CDs (the internet is the best place to look for these, too).

In both cases, it's worth the extra effort in getting a nice looking cover put together (see below) as this is really the shop window for your music. If a CD cover looks intriguing, people are more likely to pick it up and that way you're a few steps closer to making a sale.

Once you have a fully mastered copy of your CD and your artwork together, it's merely a case of sending both off to the pressing plant, paying the fee (at current prices a 'good' quote would be in the region of 38–39p per CD, but it varies enormously) and sitting back to wait for delivery – often around two weeks.

**Q:** What is MCPS?

**A:** It stands for the Mechanical Copyright Protection Society and is a body set up to ensure that songwriters and composers get paid a royalty when their music is reproduced via mechanical means. This includes printed music or other artists covering your material on their CDs.

For more information, go to their website at www.mcps-prs-alliance.co.uk.

**Q:** How do I get a cover designed for my CD?

**A:** In my view, it's worth going to a professional designer, as it's not quite as straightforward as merely knocking

something together at home on your computer. It will add to your recording budget, but it's worth it as a good looking cover is worth a great deal in the marketplace.

Many CD pressing plants have downloadable 'templates' in pro software like QuarkXpress or Adobe InDesign and include info on exactly what they require in terms of file size, picture quality and so on that will act as guidelines for your designer.

Make sure that everything you give your designer is top quality – blotchy 35mm snaps of you taken on holiday in Tenerife simply won't do if you want your product to be taken seriously. Take the time to get some good quality photos taken and be guided by your design team as to what is needed. Once again, it's a question of sitting down and discussing what you want – go into the initial meeting armed with a couple of examples of album covers you like, or give them a rough drawing. Basically, do anything to ensure that you end up with a design that is satisfying on every level.

You will need to provide the text for your cover yourself – track titles, timings, who you want to thank, details of where the CD was recorded, by whom and with what. Look at albums in your collection to see the sort of thing that people have included on their covers. Copy the legal jargon about not copying your CD, too – you want it to end up looking as professional as possible.

After you've amassed your text – and it is purely on a personal level that I ask this – please spell check it! I've seen so many album covers with silly spelling mistakes on and it really does drag a product down, in my opinion. You have the chance to make sure everything is right before it goes to press and so take it – let several people see the cover to make sure you haven't missed anything and only let it go once you're absolutely sure that it's spot on.

**Q:** Do I need to have a cover designed for a demo CD?

**A:** No, it's probably an unnecessary expense. Apart from the music, your demo's priority should really be to clearly relay information about the band – contact details, including phone numbers, email and website addresses. The ideal place for all this information is where the 'cover' of the CD should be and is probably best used in this respect rather than anything costly.

**Q:** Do I need a barcode on my CD?

**A:** If you intend trying to get your CD distributed to shops or some stores on line then a bar code is essential. Unfortunately, it's a fairly expensive business as the bar code and its accompanying 13- or 14-digit code has to be unique so it's linkable to your CD and yours alone. So you will probably find that you have to apply for a barcode from one of the suppliers that you'll find on line. Failing that, it's quite likely that the CD pressing plant will offer to supply one at an extra cost. At time of writing this cost is around £100 or so – but it's worth paying in the long term, rather than have a store refuse to stock your CD merely because it hasn't got a barcode on it.

**Q:** With recording software getting cheaper and cheaper these days, is it worth me investing in some with a view to recording an album?

**A:** I'd say no, for two reasons. One, learning any new software involves a long and tedious learning curve which is going to get in the way of you and recording your music, possibly adding a lot of additional frustration and tail-chasing in the process, too. Secondly, I believe that when you're recording, you need to be in an entirely different type of creative zone, from both temperamental and psychological points of view – and pressing buttons and messing around with levels, etc, certainly doesn't help you maintain this.

Consider also the fact that there are many peripherals to the whole recording experience – top quality studio microphones, instrument preamps, recording quality outboard effects and so on – and all these add to the basic cost of the software involved. You've also got to consider acoustics, too – and your bedroom or living space might not be optimum for recording that sax solo on the second verse! If you take all of this into account and add up the costs involved, it might even work out that booking some time in a studio is the more cost effective option, after all.

When I recorded my album, I decided that I was quite willing to pay an engineer to record it for me, leaving me free to sit there and come up with the best possible performance of the material that I could. Believe me, I'm very glad I did, as it proved that I had more than enough to worry about, just trying to access my 'muse'!

This brings us neatly around to some specific questions directed at the whole studio experience, which I passed on to studio engineer Martin Holmes, who records CDs and audio video packages for many different outlets – including my own CD.

**Q:** What does a studio engineer do?

**A:** 'First and foremost the engineer is the guy who knows how everything in the studio works and he's there to ensure the band or performer gets their music properly recorded. Beyond that, an engineer might be required to perform any number of functions depending on the nature of the session – so the job demands a flexible and resourceful approach.

Obviously, there's quite a bit of technical stuff to sort out, such as setting up the mics and patching the equipment together, but there's also a degree of 'people management' to be taken into account. When choosing a studio for your session it's worth having a chat with the engineer to see if they seem helpful and positive.'

**Q:** What's the best way for a band or performer to behave in the studio?

**A:** 'Time in the studio can be expensive and so you need to make sure you're properly prepared. It's a good idea to re-string your guitars a few days before the session so they have time to settle-in – and take the time to check that the instrument's intonation is spot-on, too. Contrary to popular belief, no amount of processing can fix an out-of-tune guitar part once it's been recorded.

It's also very important that you've rehearsed your material properly and that you can play all your parts cleanly and fluently. If there's anything you're having problems with then consider simplifying the line or phrase to make it playable. The golden rule is that simple parts played well sound much, much better than complicated ones played badly.'

**Q:** Is the engineer responsible for mixing, too?

**A:** 'On big budget sessions where the record label is picking up the tab it's not uncommon for the producer to bring in specialist mix-engineers to work on the material. In most small studios the house engineer will work with the band or performer to produce the final mix.'

**Q:** What happens in a mix?

**A:** 'Mixing is the stage where all the recorded parts are brought together and melded into a single, finished track. The specific tasks involved will differ depending on the material being mixed but usually the process involves adjusting the relevant volumes of the parts so that they work together in a pleasing way. To help achieve this, varying amounts of compression, equalisation and reverb are used to manipulate the individual character of each part and help it fit in as part of the whole.

It's definitely worth having a goal in mind when starting to mix a track, as it's all too easy to get lost along the way. Many people find it helps to keep comparing their developing mix to a commercially produced track with a similar overall sound.'

**Q:** How does mixing differ from mastering?

**A:** 'Mastering is the last stage in the process where the mixed tracks are given a final dose of compression, limiting and equalisation. Strictly speaking, the difference between mixing and mastering is that when mixing you are focusing on the individual balance of the parts within a track, whereas when mastering you are focussing on how the mixed tracks fit together as a compilation.

Mastering is a specialist job that requires its own particular approach and discipline. No two studios have identical sounding monitor systems, so to avoid any possible imbalances due to inaccurate monitoring it's advisable to have your material mastered in a different studio to where you mixed the tracks and preferably by someone who has plenty of experience.'

**Q:** Who is in charge of a session, the band, the producer or the engineer?

**A:** 'Who takes charge will depend more on the characters of the people involved, rather than any hard and fast rules. If the project has a single 'producer' then they will probably be the person with the final say. Smaller budget projects without specific producers tend to work in a more democratic fashion, with the members of the band and the engineer agreeing the plan of action amongst themselves.'

**Q:** How long does the average session last?

**A:** 'Different studios and engineers keep different hours. In general you'd expect any single session to last the length of a working day, although whether that session starts at 9am or 9pm is something you'll have to agree with the studio in question!

It's not uncommon for sessions to slog on through the night, which is undoubtedly the rock'n'roll way of doing things – but care should be taken that studio-fatigue doesn't lead to shoddy performances.'

**Q:** What are the advantages of digital recording?

**A:** 'Before the advent of digital recording everything had to be recorded using analogue tape, which was expensive and relatively difficult to use. These days you can get everything you need from a moderately powered computer with a little bit of specialist hardware and software. The upshot is that it's perfectly possible for a band or performer to record their own material at home with very little initial outlay. These developments have turned the recording industry on its head and have allowed the production of some very interesting music that would never have been possible using expensive tape technology.'

**Q:** Has anybody ever worked out what the frequency range of a guitar is when measured in Hertz? I've been told it's a lot lower down the audible frequency range than we would imagine but can't find any reference to it in books.

**A:** The audible range, as far as we humans are concerned, starts at 20Hz and rises to 20,000Hz or thereabouts, depending on age and how much time you spent listening to Motörhead as a teenager.

The frequency range of a guitar tuned conventionally starts with the low E, which clocks in at 82Hz, whilst the E at the 12th fret, top string is 659Hz. If we take it up to the higher notes, the C at the 20th fret on the top string registers 1047Hz, whilst a top E on a 24 fret instrument will deliver 1318Hz.

So much for the notes themselves – but remember that these measurements represent the fundamental frequencies and don't take into account the upper harmonics present in all notes.

# APPENDIX 1: MANAGEMENT

*There comes a time when bands start thinking about management – quite often based on the fact that they are not businessmen, they're musicians and would rather delegate the responsibilities of running the band to another individual to give them the opportunity to focus entirely on the music alone.*

*In order to field some questions about management in general, I contacted James Taylor, who manages the jazz guitarist Martin Taylor and the band Deacon Blue, amongst others...*

**Q:** When do I need to start thinking about management?

**A:** 'It's a very personal thing. Some artists like to do all their own management and others want nothing at all to do with the business side.

In the early stages of a band's career, an enthusiastic friend/dad/relative can be just as effective as a traditional manager. It would be rare to find any artist signed to a major record company who doesn't have a manager, though.'

**Q:** What does a manger do?

**A:** 'Managers have multiple roles. The main one is to act as a buffer between the artist and record companies, publishers, agents and fans.

The second is to manage the business side of the artist's career and help guide the artist's development. In the USA it is also common to have both a personal manager and a business manager. The personal manager takes care of diaries and the artist's requirements, whilst the business manager covers the financial dealings surrounding the artist.'

**Q:** What's the difference between a manager and an agent?

**A:** 'A manager manages an artist's career, which can include getting record, publishing and endorsement deals as well as liaising with the agent.

The agent simply takes care of the 'live' part of an artist's career (tours, festivals, public appearances, etc). You would normally have only one manager, but might have different agents handling different countries.

The manager co-ordinates all the agents' activities.'

**www.P3music.com**

# APPENDIX 2:
# PUBLIC RELATIONS & PUBLICITY

*You've recorded your CD and so the next step is to alert the public at large to its existence. Ad campaigns in national press and magazines is an extremely costly business and generally open only to the major league. But there are other ways of securing those precious column inches...*

**Q:** How do I get my CD reviewed in magazines and newspapers?

**A:** If you are not engaging a pro publicist to assist, you, this can be a hit or miss process, to say the least. At one time, it used to be that if your CD was not going to be available at retail outlets then magazines would be a little dubious about reviewing it. But now that web commerce is becoming more and more commonplace, this shouldn't be an issue today. I say 'shouldn't' but you might still find some publications who are attached to the old way of thinking, so don't expect miracles.

Basically, to begin with you need to get some sort of press pack together. This can be as simple as a press release and a biog of the artist or band or as all singing, all dancing as you can make it. But bear in mind all the way through that journalists don't have a lot of time and so sending in something the size of War And Peace probably isn't going to get read. Journalists like something that gets straight to the point and tells them everything they need to know about an artist and their latest CD as quickly, neatly and efficiently as possible.

So don't waffle – just deal with the facts. If you're not good at writing, it's a good idea to find someone who is and get them to write a press release for you – in all honesty, badly written biogs, press releases, etc usually enjoy a one way trip to the waste bin, in my experience. Anything that takes undue effort to read or understand isn't worth spending time with – and it probably has the effect of dragging down your professionally recorded masterpiece to an amateur level at the same time. Remember, you're in competition with major league artists who have massive publicity budgets at their disposal and so every word counts.

Try to avoid exaggerating your or your band's talents, but don't be negative at the same time. Find a balance and tell the truth – if you've sent in a press release that claims that you're the new Metallica and you're not even close, then it's not going to win you any friends in the press. Music journalists get to listen to a lot of music and can soon spot a fake or a feeble 'wannabe' effort – so use common sense and discretion here.

Don't make outrageous claims in your biog, either; I've read some absolute twaddle in my years as a journalist, with people claiming to have worked with so-and-so and played at such-and-such a gig, whereas it's fairly obvious that it's just a case of the hyperbole fairy working overtime!

The next thing to do is to find out which publications are likely to review your CD and target them accordingly. I don't have to tell you that it's no good sending a heavy rock magnum opus to a magazine that specialises in roots, world and folk music – or do I? Do your research; spend some time in a newsagent, looking through the music titles and then make a note of the addresses of those who you think might look favourably upon your type of music. Go to the websites and see if you can track down any more insight – it's best to be sure in these cases as a misfired promo CD is a waste of everyone's time.

It's sometimes best to phone a magazine and ask who is in charge of the CD reviews and then you've got a name to put on the envelope. If in doubt, send it to the editor – and it's worth an extra couple of points if you take the time to find out his or her name first, too!

Load up your CD, press release, etc in a sufficiently padded jiffy bag (you'd be shocked, distressed and amazed at how many damaged CDs I used to receive through the post when I worked on the magazines) and send them off. There's no hurry in these instances, and so you could save yourself a bob or two by sending all your promo CDs out via second class post.

The next thing to mention is that it takes time for a review to appear in a magazine. Publications have what's known as a 'lead in' time, which is the approximate amount of time it takes to get a feature or article published, thanks to production schedules and printing, etc. Ours used to be around eight weeks – yes, that's two months – and so patience is going to have to be factored into your press campaign somewhere.

The big record companies usually release advance copies of albums in order to combat the time-lag of lead in times. So we would receive a preview copy up to six or eight weeks ahead of general release so that the review was pretty much simultaneous with the CD appearing in the shops. Needless to say, this isn't a luxury that a small budget affair can usually stretch to and so you'll just have to put up with it and wait.

It is a good idea to follow your CD up with a polite phone call to ask if a review is at all likely. Magazines get sent hundreds of CDs a month and so anything you can do to bring yours nearer the top of the 'probable' list is well worth the effort. Whether your call will help or hinder your chances, of course, is down to your skills on the phone. Professional press people are very good at this and know exactly how to treat a busy journalist in order to get results. Furthermore, they've probably had the chance to build up a relationship with most of the guys and gals on the magazines through experience... But if you're going in cold, whatever you do don't resort to the rock'n'roll cliché and try to act 'cool' because journalists haven't got time for it – and your CD will hit the bin. Be polite, straight to the point – ask if they've received the CD and if they've had a chance to listen to it yet. If not, ask if it would be OK to call back in a week's time, or something like that.

A lot of this sounds a little hit or miss and unfortunately, it is. It's never easy to get your music publicised and if your CD is essentially an 'independent' release, then the task is a lot harder. Don't give up, though, because a favourable review from a respected magazine or journalist can be absolute gold dust in terms of publicity.

## Q: How do I get my music played on the radio?

**A:** If your CD is your own independent release, then it's wise to start with some local radio stations. Look them up on the internet or a local source (local radio stations are never backward about making their presence known!) and investigate which DJ plays anything close to your style of music. Then, send in a CD with your press pack to that DJ by name, possibly following the mailing up with either a phone call or email (a lot of DJs will now respond to email whilst they are on the air) to see if they've received it and if they are likely to play a track. If there is some additional 'local' interest, like you have a gig coming up or something, plug this too as local events are generally high on the agenda and considered newsworthy by radio staff. Don't forget your local BBC radio station, too – listener figures tend to be less than the commercial stations, but there's definitely some kudos to be had from being able to quote the Beeb on your press release.

If you are playing gigs in other areas then it's a good idea to repeat the process outlined above in whichever area you're going to be playing. You won't always be successful, but it's certainly worth trying.

*The deluxe route in PR is to employ a specialist to promote your CD and/or tour. In order to answer the next series of questions, I asked Sue Williams from Frontier Promotions, an established PR company based in Norfolk, to shine a light on pro PR.*

**Q:** What does a PR person do?

**A:** 'Represent an artist by promoting their album, single or tour. If we are promoting gigs we send releases with biogs, tour dates and photos to national and local press, then follow through to try to get reviews and features.'

**Q:** Who employs the PR, the artist or record company?

**A:** 'Both – and sometimes a management company or agent may employ a publicist, too.'

**Q:** What's the key to getting new CDs reviewed in the media?

**A:** 'Patience, persistence and the promotion company having a reputation for always representing good music.'

**Q:** How can an artist help in promotion?

**A:** 'By furnishing the PR company with a good biography of themselves with as much information about where they come from, their influences – and being available for interviews when asked to do them.'

**Q:** What are the dos and don'ts as far as PR is concerned?

**A:** 'Try to keep the door and options open as long as you can whilst you are building an artist's profile but don't overstay your welcome. Always respect the review or features editors and only argue when you are really convinced they are wrong – otherwise they will not entertain you next time.'

**Q:** Is it possible for an artist to do his or her own PR?

**A:** 'Yes, but not advisable because there are millions of releases now and the chances of getting through to the media are very small. Having a PR company representing you will get you one step further up that very long ladder.'

# APPENDIX 3: RECORD DEALS

*It used to be true that getting a record deal was the only way of releasing your material to the public at large. Major league record companies these days tend to place more emphasis on the 'easy buck' rather than having any philanthropic or artistic leanings – hence the never-ending spew of glittery teenage pop, parasitically linked to insidious fashion trends. Me, bitter? God, no...*

**Q: Is there an alternative to getting a record deal?**

**A:** I believe there is, yes. Thanks to the fact that CDs are now relatively easy and cheap to produce a whole 'cottage industry' has begun to grow outside of, and completely detached from, the mainstream record industry. This enables an artist or band to record a CD and go out on the road to promote it at gigs or via the internet (or preferably both!) without the constraints or profit-absorbing administrations of big business.

I think this is a healthy thing for music in general as it's a system that is basically open to all, unlike the notoriously fickle and horribly fashion-based music industry.

It also overrules some of the more ridiculous whimsy that the music industry is known for – I know of one excellently capable guitarist who was turned down for a position in a big touring pop band because he was 'too tall'. Go figure.

Touring and selling your own self-produced work might not appear to be quite as glamorous as the traditional rock'n'roll routes open only to the chosen few, but it's a way to earn a living from professional music that simply wasn't available to any of us a comparatively short while ago.

It's hard work, but ultimately, you remain your own boss and more in charge of your musical destiny than you would be if enslaved by the major league!

**Q: I've made a CD with my band – what's the best way of selling it to the public?**

**A:** I think your first resource these days is the internet. If you're at all serious about promoting your band and its music, you are virtually dead in the water without a website of your own. Furthermore, a website provides an excellent base from which to promote gigs and sell CDs – or give 'tasters' of your music in the form of downloadable mp3s.

If you decide to set up some kind of web-based 'shop' you'll have to investigate web commerce, where you can accept credit and debit card transactions online. There are plenty of companies who will host such a resource for you (at a cost, obviously) and a little bit of research will yield some quotes as to how much this will cost you. Whatever you do, don't rely on the old 'cheques sent to a PO Box number' route because people just don't buy their CDs that way any more. If someone who is a potential customer finds your website, they are far more likely to order a CD if they can do so immediately via a secure connection.

There are other alternatives available – some sites like www.guitarcds.net will sell your CD for you for a percentage of the sale have the advantage of an established online presence with a secure transaction capability already set up.

Failing that, the only way to get your CD available in high street stores is to negotiate a distribution deal, but distributors cost money and, once again, this might not prove to be cost-effective for a low budget operation.

*If you want to go the more traditional route of sending your CD or demo into a record company in the hope that they will 'sign you up', then there is a strategy in place for that, too. To answer questions here, I once again went to James Taylor at P3 Music (www.p3music.com) who runs The Guitar Label.*

## Q: Do you like to receive demos?

**A:** 'Only if it is music we are interested in. It gets very boring receiving demos by dance music artists when we (i.e. P3 Music and The Guitar Label) deal predominantly with guitar music!

When you send out your demo you must really target it because the scatter gun effect wastes both your time and that of the record company.'

## Q: How is it best for a band/performer to present themselves to a record company?

**A:** 'I like it when an artist is recommended by someone I trust, such as an agent, promoter or lawyer. If an agent comes to me saying they have an artist they are working with who is selling out shows, that gets me interested. I would always say to an artist to get their live side sorted out first because it instantly puts you on the top of the pile.

Also, artists could benefit from getting mentoring from other artists. If you can build up a friendship with an artist who has achieved some success it can really speed up your learning of the music business and increase your chances of success.

# INDEX

1 2 3 4 5 6 7 8 9